A Selected Bibliography of Virginia

❧

1607–169?

E. G. Swem and John M. Jennings

CLEARFIELD COMPANY

Originally Published 1957

Reprinted for
Clearfield Company, Inc. by
Genealogical Publishing Company Inc.
Baltimore, Maryland
1994

International Standard Book Number 0-8063-4514-4

*Jamestown 350th Anniversary Historical Booklet
Number 1*

TABLE OF CONTENTS

FOREWORD

This bibliography is a modest collection of titles relating to the life of seventeenth-century Virginia in its broadest interpretation. It has been compiled with the need in mind of the general reader and of the student who is just beginning research in the alluring field of early Virginia history. Numerous titles have been omitted for the reason that the number of pages allotted to this booklet requires forbearance and retrenchment. The earnest purpose of the compilers has been to include a good representation of those books and contributions in periodicals that have stood the test of time. Again, yielding to the demands of economy, the titles have been reduced in length from the full style followed in standard catalogue entries. There is enough information included in each title to enable the consultant to judge of the contents of the book to which the title refers, and to learn its date and size; enough to whet his historical appetite and to cause him to hasten with joy to the nearest college or reference library, where he will receive a happy welcome and be shown the books he wishes in original edition, in reprint, or in reproduced form of photostat, microfilm, microcard, or microsheet.

The arrangement of titles has been designed for browsing: secondary works are arranged by author under certain general subjects; primary materials, following collections of original narratives, by date from "before 1607" to 1699.

The senior editors wish to acknowledge the cordial cooperation of Miss Spotswood Hunnicutt, and to extend to our collaborator, Mr. James A. Servies, Reference Librarian of William and Mary College, warm gratitude and high praise for the characteristic industry and enthusiasm he has displayed in every step of this compilation. His rare gift of discerning bibliographical values has been constantly in evidence.

VIRGINIA.

A
SERMON
PREACHED AT

WHITE-CHAPPEL, IN THE
prefence of many, Honourable and
Worfhipfull, the Adventurers and Planters for VIRGINIA.
25 April, 1609.

PVBLISHED FOR THE BENEFIT

AND VSE OF THE COLONY, PLANTED,
and to bee Planted there, and for the Ad-
uancement of their CHRIS-
TIAN Purpofe.

By WILLIAM SYMONDS, Preacher at Saint
SAVIOURS in Southwarke.

IVDE. 22. 23.
Haue compaffion of fome, in putting of difference:
And other faue with feare, pulling them out of the fire.

LONDON:

Printed by I. WINDET for ELEAZAR EDGAR, and
William Welby, and are to be fold in Paules Church-
yard at the Signe of the Windmill.
1609.

Nova Britannia.
OFFRING MOST
Excellent fruites by Planting in
Virginia

Exciting all ſuch as be well affected
to further the ſame.

London
Printed for Samvel Macham, and are to be ſold at
his Shop in Pauls Church-yard, at the
Signe of the Bul-head.
1 6 0 9.

NEVVES FROM VIRGINIA.

THE LOST FLOCKE TRIUMPHANT;

With the happy Arrival of that famous and
worthy knight Sr Thomas Gates : and
the well reputed and valient Captaine Mr Christopher New-
porte, and others, into
Virginia.

With the manner of their distresse in the Iland of **Devils**
(otherwise called Bermoothawes) where they
remained 42 weeks, and builded
two Pynaces, in which
they returned unto
Virginia.

---

by R. RICH, GENT., one of the voyage.

LONDON:

Printed by Edw. Allde, and are to be solde by John
Wright, at Christ-Church dore. 1610.

A TRVE

DISCOVRSE OF THE

PRESENT ESTATE OF VIR-
GINIA, and the fucceſſe of the affaires
there till the 18 of *Iune.* 1614.
TOGETHER.

WITH A RELATION OF THE
feuerall Engliſh Townes and fortes, the aſſu-
red hopes of that countrie and the peace
concluded with the Indians.

The Chriſtening of *Powhatans* daughter
and her marriage with an Engliſh-man.

Written by RAPHE HAMOR the yon-
ger, late Secretarie in that Colony.

Alget, qui non ardet.

Printed at London by IOHN BEALE for WIL-
LIAM WELBY dwelling at the figne of the
Swanne in Pauls Church-yard 1615.

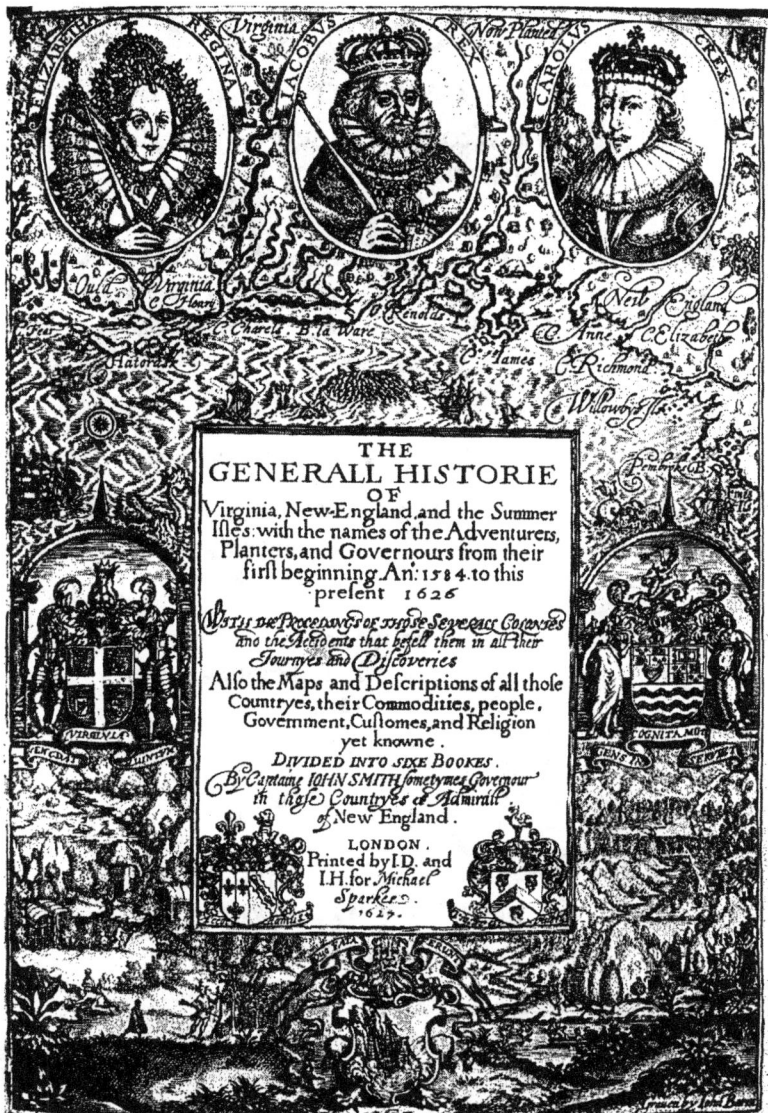

THE
GENERALL HISTORIE
OF
Virginia, New-England, and the Summer
Isles: with the names of the Adventurers,
Planters, and Governours from their
first beginning. An: 1584. to this
present 1626

WITH THE PROCEEDINGS OF THOSE SEVERALL COLONIES
and the Accidents that befell them in all their
Journyes and Discoveries

Also the Maps and Descriptions of all those
Countryes, their Commodities, people,
Government, Customes, and Religion
yet knowne.
DIVIDED INTO SIXE BOOKES.
By Captaine IOHN SMITH sometymes Governour
in those Countryes & Admirall
of New England.

LONDON.
Printed by I.D. and
I.H. for Michael
Sparkes.
1627.

VIRGINIA

Impartially examined, and left to publick view, to be confidered by all Iudicious and honeft men.

Under which Title, is comprehended the Degrees from 34 to 39, wherein lyes the rich and healthfull Countries of *Roanook*, the now Plantations of *Virginia* and *Mary-land*.

Looke not upon this BOOKE, as thofe that are fet out by private men, for private ends; for being read, you'l find, the publick good is the Authors onely aime.

For this Piece is no other then the Adventurers or Planters faithfull Steward, difpofing the Adventure for the beft advantage, advifing people of all degrees, from the higheft Mafter, to the meaneft Servant, how fuddenly to raife their fortunes.

Perufe the Table, and you fhall finde the way plainely layd downe

By WILLIAM BVLLOCK, Gent.

19 *April*, 1649. *Jmprimatur*, Hen: Whaley.

LONDON:

Printed by *John Hammond*, and are to be fold at his houfe over-againft S. *Andrews* Church in *Holborne*. 1649.

VIRGINIA:

More especially the South part thereof, Richly and truly valued: *viz*.

The fertile *Carolana*, and no leſſe excellent Iſle of *Roanoak*, of Latitude from 31. to 37. Degr. relating the meanes of rayſing infinite profits to the Adventurers and Planters.

The ſecond Edition, with Addition of

THE DISCOVERY OF SILKWORMS,
with their benefit.

And Implanting of Mulberry Trees.

ALSO
The Dreſſing of Vines , for the rich Trade of making Wines in VIRGINIA.

Together with
The making of the Saw-mill, very uſefull in *Virginia*, for cutting of Timber and Clapbord to build withall, and its Converſion to many as profitable Uſes.

By *E. W.* Gent.

LONDON,
Printed by *T. H.* for *John Stephenson*, at the Signe of the Sun below Ludgate. 1650.

PUBLICK
GOOD
Without Private
INTEREST.
OR,

A Compendious *Remonstrance* of the present sad State and Condition of the English Colonie in V I R G I N E A.

WITH

A Modest D E C L A R A T I O N of the severall Causes (so far as by the Rules of Right, Reason, and Religious Obser- vation may be Collected) why it hath not prospered better hitherto

AS ALSO,

A Submissive suggestion of the most prudentiall probable wayes. and meanes, both Divine and Civill (that the inexpert Remembrancer could for the present recall to minde) for its happyer improvement and advancement for the future.

Humbly presented to His Highness the Lord *Protectour*, By a Person zealously devoted, To the more effectual propagating of the Gospel in that Nation, and to the inlargement of the Honour and Benefit, both of the said Colonie, and this whole Nation, from whence they have been transplanted.

Qui sibi solium se natum putat,
secum solus semper vivat,
Hoc solum habent homines cum deo commune,
Aliu bene facere Synes.
To do good, and to communicate, forget not:
for with such sacrifices, God is well pleased, *Heb.* 13.v.16.

L O N D O N,
Printed for *Henry Marsh*, and are to be sold at the Crown in S. *Paul's* Church-yard. 1657.

BIBLIOGRAPHIES AND GUIDES

ABBOT, WILLIAM W. A Virginia chronology, 1585-1783. Williamsburg, 1957. (Jamestown 350th anniversary historical booklet, No. 2.)

ASSOCIATION FOR PRESERVATION of Virginia Antiquities. Yearbook. Richmond, 1896-date.

BROCK, ROBERT A. Virginia, 1606-1689 [with a critical essay on the sources of information]. In: Winsor, Narrative and critical history, v. 3, p. 127-68.

BROWN UNIVERSITY. John Carter Brown library. Bibliotheca Americana; catalogue of the . . . library. Providence, R. I., 1919-1931. 3 v.

COLE, GEORGE W. A catalogue of books relating to the discovery and early history of North and South America forming a part of the library of E. D. Church. N. Y., 1907. 5 v.

EAMES, WILBERFORCE. A bibliography of Captain John Smith. N. Y., 1927. 48 p.

[KENNETT, WHITE]. Bibliothecae Americanae primordia. An attempt towards laying the foundation of an American library. London, 1713. 283 p.

KINGSBURY, SUSAN M. An introduction to the records of the Virginia company of London with a bibliographical list of the extant documents. Washington, 1905. 214 p.

> Reprinted: Kingsbury, Records of the Virginia company, v. 1, p. 11-206.

NEW YORK (CITY). Public Library. List of works in the New York public library relating to Virginia. N. Y., 1907. 71 p.

PHILLIPS, PHILIP L. List of books relating to America in the

1

register of the London company of stationers, from 1562-1638. Am. hist. assoc., Report (1896), v. 1, p. 1249-61.

_____Virginia cartography; a bibliographical description. Washington, 1896. 85 p. (Smithsonian institution publication, no. 1039)

SABIN, JOSEPH. Bibliotheca Americana. A dictionary of books relating to America, from its discovery to the present time. N. Y., 1868-1936. 29 v.

STANARD, WILLIAM G. The colonial Virginia register. Albany, N. Y., 1902. 249 p.

_____The Virginia archives. Am. hist. assoc., Report, 1903, v. 1, p. 645-64.

SWEM, EARL G. Bibliography of Virginia. Richmond, 1916-19. 3 v.

_____Maps relating to Virginia in the Virginia state library. Richmond, 1914. [33]-263 p. (Virginia state library, Bulletin, v. 7, nos. 2-3.)

_____Virginia historical index. Roanoke, Va., 1934-36. 2 v.

TORRENCE, WILLIAM C. A trial bibliography of colonial Virginia. Richmond, 1908-10. 2 v. (Virginia state library, 5th-6th report, 1908-10.)

VIRGINIA HISTORICAL SOCIETY. Catalogue of the manuscripts. Richmond, 1901. 120 p.

VIRGINIA STATE LIBRARY. Calendar of transcripts [in the Virginia State Library]. Richmond, 1905. 658, xliv p.

WINSOR, JUSTIN. Maryland and Virginia [with a critical bibliography]. In his: Narrative and critical history, v. 5, p. 259-84.

2

SECONDARY WORKS

U. S. HISTORY—INCLUDING HISTORY OF THE SOUTH

ANDREWS, CHARLES M. The Colonial period of American history. New Haven, Conn., 1934-38. 4 v.

_____Our earliest colonial settlements, their diversities of origin and later characteristics. N. Y., 1933. 179 p.

AVERY, ELROY M. A history of the United States and its people. Cleveland, 1904-10. 7 v.

BANCROFT, GEORGE. A history of the United States. Boston, 1834-74. 10 v.

BEER, GEORGE L. The old colonial system, 1660-1754. N. Y., 1912. 2 v.

_____The origins of the British colonial system, 1578-1660. N. Y., 1908. 438 p.

BOLTON, HERBERT E. AND T. M. MARSHALL. The colonization of North America, 1492-1783. N. Y., 1920. 609 p.

BOND, BEVERLY W. The quit-rent system in the American colonies. New Haven, Conn., 1919. 492 p.

BOZMAN, JOHN L. The history of Maryland, from its first settlement in 1633, to the restoration, in 1660. Baltimore, 1837. 2 v.

BRISTOL AND AMERICA, a record of the first settlers in the colonies of North America, 1654-1685. London, 1929. 182 p.

THE CAMBRIDGE HISTORY of the British empire. v. 1, The old empire from the beginnings to 1783. Cambridge, 1929. 931 p.

CHALMERS, GEORGE. Political annals of the present united col-

3

onies, from their settlement to the peace of 1763. Book 1, London, 1780. 695 p.

Book 2 published in N. Y. hist. soc., Collections (Publication fund ser.), 1 (1868), 1-176.

CHANNING, EDWARD. A history of the United States. N. Y., 1905-25. 6 v.

v. 1, "The planting of a nation in the new world, 1000-1660."
v. 2, "A century of colonial history, 1660-1760."

CHATTERTON, EDWARD K. English seamen and the colonization of America. London, 1930. 326 p.

CHITWOOD, OLIVER P. A history of colonial America. 2nd ed. N. Y., 1948. 874 p.

CRANE, VERNER W. The Southern frontier, 1670-1732. Durham, N. C., 1928. 391 p.

CRAVEN, WESLEY F. The southern colonies in the seventeenth century, 1607-1689. Baton Rouge, La., 1949. 451 p.

[CROUCH, NATHANIEL] A seventeenth century survey of America. [A reprint of "The English empire in America," 3rd ed., 1698.] Prepared by the personnel of the Work projects administration, San Francisco, Calif., 1940. 124 p.

DODD, WILLIAM E. The old South; struggles for democracy. N. Y., 1937. 312 p.

DOUGLASS, WILLIAM. A summary, historical and political, of the first planting, progressive improvements, and present state of the British settlements in North America, Boston, 1755. 2 v.

DOYLE, JOHN A. English colonies in America. N. Y., 1882-1907. 5 v.

v. 1, "Virginia, Maryland and the Carolinas."

EGGLESTON, EDWARD. The transit of civilization from England to America in the seventeenth century. N. Y., 1901. 344 p.

4

GAYLEY, CHARLES M. Shakespeare and the founders of liberty in America. N. Y., 1917. 270 p.

[HALL, FAYR] A short account of the first settlement of the provinces of Virginia, Maryland, New-York, New-Jersey, and Pennsylvania, by the British. London, 1735. 22 p.

Reprinted [N. Y., 1922] 22 p.

HART, ALBERT B., ed. American history told by contemporaries. N. Y., 1901-1902. 4 v.

HOTTEN, JOHN C. The original lists of persons of quality; emigrants; religious exiles; political rebels; serving men sold for a term of years; apprentices; children stolen; maidens pressed; and others who went from Great Britain to the American plantations, 1600-1700. London, 1874. 604 p.

HUBBELL, JAY B. The South in American Literature, 1607-1900. [Durham, N. C.] 1954. 987 p.

INGRAM, ARTHUR F. W. The early English colonies; a summary [of a lecture] transcribed by Sadler Phillips. Milwaukee, Wis., 1908. 228 p.

JERNEGAN, MARCUS W. Laboring and dependent classes in colonial America, 1607-1783. Chicago [1931] 256 p.

JOHNSON, EDGAR A. J. American economic thought in the seventeenth century. London, 1932. 292 p.

JOHNSTON, MARY. Pioneers of the old South; a chronicle of English colonial beginnings. New Haven, Conn., 1921. 260 p. (Chronicles of America, v. 5)

KEITH, WILLIAM. The history of the British plantations in America. With a chronological account of the most remarkable things, which happen'd to the first adventurers . . . Part 1. Virginia. London, 1738. 187 p.

5

LABAREE, LEONARD W. Royal government in America; a study of the British colonial system before 1783. New Haven, Conn., 1930. 491 p.

LODGE, HENRY C. A short history of the English colonies in America. [Rev. ed.] N. Y., 1882. 560 p.

MORRIS, RICHARD B. Government and labor in early America. N. Y., 1946. 557 p.

____Studies in the history of American law, with special reference to the seventeenth and eighteenth centuries. N. Y., 1930. 285 p.

MORSE, JARVIS M. American beginnings: highlights and sidelights of the birth of the New World. Washington [1952] 260 p.

OSGOOD, HERBERT L. The American colonies in the seventeenth century. N. Y., 1904-1907. 3 v.

PIERCY, JOSEPHINE K. Studies in literary types in seventeenth century America (1607-1710). New Haven, Conn., 1939. 360 p. (Yale Studies in English, v. 91)

PRIESTLEY HERBERT I. The coming of the white man, 1492-1848. N. Y., 1929. 411 p.

ROBERTSON, WILLIAM. The history of America, books IX. and X. containing the history of Virginia to the year 1688; and of New England to the year 1652. Philadelphia, 1799. 196 p.

First printed 1777, often reprinted.

THE SOUTH in the building of the nation. Richmond [1903-1913]. 13 v.

TREVELYAN, GEORGE M. England under the Stuarts. 12th ed. London, 1925. 566 p.

6

Tyler, Lyon G. The Cavalier in America. [Richmond, 1913.] 19 p.

Tyler, Moses C. A history of American literature during the colonial time. N. Y., 1897. 2 v.

Wertenbaker, Thomas J. The first Americans, 1607-1690. N. Y., 1927. 358 p. (A history of American life, v. 2)

Wilson, Woodrow. A history of the American people. [New ed.] N. Y., 1917. 10 v.

Winsor, Justin, ed. Narrative and critical history of America. Boston, 1884-89. 8 v.

Wissler, Clark [and others]. Adventurers in the wilderness. New Haven, Conn., 1925. 369 p. (Pageant of America, v. 1)

Virginia History—Including Local History

Abernethy, Thomas P. Three Virginia frontiers. Baton Rouge, La., 1940. 96 p.
(The W. L. Fleming lectures in Southern history, Louisiana State Univ., 1940)

Andrews, Matthew P. Virginia, the Old Dominion. N. Y., 1937. 664 p.

Armes, Ethel M. Stratford hall, the great house of the Lees. Richmond, 1936. 575 p.

Association for the preservation of Virginia antiquities. The old lighthouse at Cape Henry, Virginia; an account of early efforts to establish a lighthouse at entrance to Chesapeake Bay, 1607, 1789, 1947. Norfolk, 1947. 16 p.

Beverley, Robert. The history of Virginia. 2nd ed. London, 1722. 284 p.
Reprinted: Richmond, 1855. 264 p.; Chapel Hill, N. C., 1947. 366 p. First ed.: London, 1705

7

BODDIE, JOHN B. Colonial Surry. Richmond, 1948. 249 p.

BRUCE, PHILIP A. [and others] History of Virginia. Chicago, 1924. 6 v.

"Colonial period, by Philip A. Bruce," v. 1.

____The Virginia Plutarch. Chapel Hill, N. C., 1929. 2 v.

BURK, JOHN D. The history of Virginia, from its first settlement to the commencement of the revolution. Petersburg, Va., 1822. 3 v.

Documents, &c. [relating to Bacon's rebellion], v. 2, p. 247-74. Papers relating to the mission for procuring a more perfect charter [1674-76], v. 2, appendix, p. xxxiii-lxii.

CAMPBELL, CHARLES. History of the colony and ancient dominion of Virginia. Philadelphia, 1860. 765 p.

CHANDLER, JULIAN A. C. AND TRAVIS B. THAMES. Colonial Virginia. Richmond, 1907. 388 p.

____Makers of Virginia history. N. Y. [1904] 347 p.

CLARK, CHARLES B. The Eastern Shore of Maryland and Virginia. N. Y., [1950] 3 v.

CONWAY, MONCURE D. Barons of the Potomack and the Rappahannock. N. Y., 1892. 290 p.

COOKE, JOHN E. Virginia; a history of the people. [New ed.] Boston, 1903. 535 p.

FISKE, JOHN. Old Virginia and her neighbors. Boston, 1900. 2 v.

FOOTE, WILLIAM H. Sketches of Virginia, historical and biographical. [1st ser.] Philadelphia, 1850. 568 p.

GILLIAM, SARA K. Virginia's people. A study of the growth and distribution of the population of Virginia from 1607 to 1943. [Richmond] 1944. 132 p.

8

GLENN, THOMAS A. Some colonial mansions and those who lived in them, with genealogies of the various families mentioned [ser. 1]. Philadelphia, 1898. 459 p.

GOODWIN, RUTHERFOORD. A brief & true report concerning Williamsburg in Virginia: being an account of the most important occurrences in that place from its first beginning to the present time. . . . 3d ed. Williamsburg [1941] 406 p.

HOWE, HENRY. Historical collections of Virginia. Charleston, S. C., 1845. 544 p.

HOWISON, ROBERT R. A history of Virginia, from its discovery and settlement by Europeans to the present time. Philadelphia, 1848. 2 v.

INGLE, EDWARD. Local institutions of Virginia. Baltimore, 1885. 127 p. (Johns Hopkins univ. stud. in hist. and pol. sci., ser. 3, no. 2-3)

JOHNSTON, FREDERICK. Memorials of old Virginia clerks . . . from 1634 to the present time. Lynchburg, 1888. 405 p.

JONES, HUGH. The present state of Virginia, from whence is inferred a short view of Maryland and North Carolina. Ed. by Richard L. Morton. Chapel Hill, N. C., [1956] 295 p.

First published in 1724; reprinted N. Y., 1865. 151 p.
KIBLER, J. LUTHER. The cradle of the nation; . . . Jamestown, Williamsburg and Yorktown. Richmond, 1931. 64 p.

MARTIN, JOSEPH. A new and comprehensive gazetteer of Virginia, and the District of Columbia . . . to which is added a history of Virginia from its first settlement to the year 1754 [by W. H. Brockenbrough]. Charlottesville, Va., 1835. 636 p.

MAURY, RICHARD L. The Huguenots in Virginia. [n.p., 1902?] 116 p.

MEADE, WILLIAM. Old churches, ministers and families of Virginia. Philadelphia, 1861. 2 v.

PAGE, THOMAS N. The Old Dominion; her making and her manners. N. Y., 1908. 394 p.

PRITTS, JOSEPH. Mirror of olden time border life; embracing a history of the discovery of America . . . Also, history of Virginia, embracing its first settlement, the progressive movements of civilization and the establishment of civil government . . . [2nd ed.] Abingdon, Va., 1849. 700 p.

ROBINSON, MORGAN P. A complete index to Stith's history of Virginia. Richmond, 1912. 152 p.

____Virginia counties. Richmond, 1916. 283 p. (Virginia state library, Bulletin, v. 9, no. 1-3)

STANARD, MARY N. Colonial Virginia, its people and customs. Philadelphia, 1917. 375 p.

STARKEY, MARION L. The first plantation; a history of Hampton and Elizabeth City county, Virginia, 1607-1887. [Hampton, Va.], 1936. 95 p.

STITH, WILLIAM. The history of the first discovery and settlement of Virginia. Williamsburg, Va., 1747. 341, 34 p.
    Reprinted: N. Y., 1865. 341, 34 p.

[TYLER, LYON G.] History of York county in the seventeenth century. Tyler's quarterly, 1 (1919), 231-75.

VIRGINIA. DEPT. OF conservation. A hornbook of Virginia history; comp. by J. R. V. Daniel. [Richmond, 1949] 141 p.

____State historical markers of Virginia. 6th ed. Richmond [1948] 262 p.

WEDDELL, ALEXANDER W. (ed.) A memorial volume of Virginia historical portraiture, 1585-1830. Richmond, 1930.

10

WERTENBAKER, THOMAS J. The old South; the founding of American civilization. N. Y., 1942. 364 p.

WHITELAW, RALPH T. Virginia's Eastern Shore. Richmond, 1951. 2 v.

WILLIS, CARRIE. The story of Virginia. rev. ed. N. Y., 1950. 392 p.

WILLISON, GEORGE F. Behold Virginia: the fifth crown. N. Y., [1951] 422 p.

WRITERS' PROGRAM, VIRGINIA. Virginia; a guide to the Old Dominion. N. Y. [1940] 710 p.

SIXTEENTH-CENTURY VIRGINIA

LEWIS, CLIFFORD M. AND ALBERT J. LOOMIE. The Spanish Jesuit mission in Virginia, 1570-1572. Chapel Hill, N. C., 1953. 294 p.

LORANT, STEFAN, ed. The new world; the first pictures of America by John White and Jacques Le Moyne and engraved by Theodore De Bry, with contemporary narratives of the Huguenot settlement in Florida, 1562-1565, and the Virginia colony, 1585-1590. N. Y., 1946. 292 p.

MOOK, MAURICE A. The aboriginal population of Tidewater Virginia. Am. anthropologist (new ser.), 46 (1944), 193-208.

SAMS, CONWAY W. The conquest of Virginia: the first attempt. Norfolk, Va., 1924. 547 p.

TARBOX, INCREASE N. Sir Walter Ralegh and his colony in America. Including the charter of Queen Elizabeth in his favor, March 25, 1584, with letters, discourses, and narratives of the voyages made to America at his charges, and descriptions of the country, commodities, and inhabitants. Boston, 1885. 329 p. (Prince society publications, v. 15)

11

ALVORD, CLARENCE W. AND LEE BIDGOOD. The first explorations of the trans-Allegheny region by the Virginians, 1650-1674. Cleveland, 1912. 275 p.

AMES, SUSIE M. Studies of the Virginia Eastern Shore in the seventeenth century. Richmond, 1940. 274 p.

ANDREWS, MATTHEW P. The soul of a nation; the founding of Virginia and the projection of New England. N. Y., 1943. 378 p.

BODDIE, JOHN B. Seventeenth-century Isle of Wight county, Virginia. Chicago [1938] 756 p.

BRITTINGHAM, JOSEPH B. The first trading post at Kicotan (Kecoughtan) Hampton, Virginia. Hampton, 1947. 23 p.

BROWN, ALEXANDER. The first republic in America; an account of the origin of this nation, written from the records then (1624) concealed by the Council, rather than from the histories then licensed by the Crown. Boston, 1898. 688 p.

____The genesis of the United States. A narrative of the movement in England, 1605-1616, which resulted in the plantation of North America by Englishmen. Boston, 1890. 2 v. "Brief biographies," v. 2, p. 811-1068.

____New views of early Virginia history, 1606-1619. Liberty, Va., 1886. 18 p.

BRUCE, PHILIP A. The economic and social life of Virginia in the seventeenth century. In: The South in the building of the nation, v. 1, p. 46-73.

CHANDLER, JULIAN A. C. The beginnings of Virginia, 1584-1624. In: The South in the building of the nation, v. 1, p. 1-23.

12

CHEYNEY, EDWARD P. Some conditions surrounding the settlement of Virginia. Am. hist. rev., 12 (1907), 507-28.

CRAVEN, WESLEY F. Dissolution of the Virginia company; the failure of a colonial experiment. N. Y., 1932. 350 p.

____The Virginia company of London, 1606-1624. Williamsburg, 1957. (Jamestown 350th anniversary historical booklet, No. 5.)

DODD, WILLIAM E. The emergence of the first social order in the United States. Am. hist. rev., 40 (1935), 217-31.

[ELLYSON, JAMES T.] The London company of Virginia; a brief account of its transactions in colonizing Virginia. N. Y., 1908. 24 p.

FORMAN, HENRY C. The architecture of the Old South: the medieval style, 1585-1850. Cambridge, Mass., 1948. 203 p.

____Virginia architecture in seventeenth century. Williamsburg, 1957. (Jamestown 350th anniversary historical booklet, No. 11.)

GREEN, BENNETT W. How Newport's News got its name. Richmond, 1907. 142 p.

GREER, GEORGE C. Early Virginia immigrants [1623-1666] Richmond, 1912. 376 p.

HARTWELL, HENRY. The present state of Virginia, and the college, by Henry Hartwell, James Blair, and Edward Chilton [1727]. Ed. by Hunter D. Farish. Williamsburg, Va., 1940. lxxiii, 105 p.

HENRY, WILLIAM W. The settlement at Jamestown, with particular reference to the late attacks upon Captain John Smith, Pocahontas, and John Rolfe. Va. hist. soc., Proceedings, 1882, p. 10-63.

13

JEFFERSON, THOMAS. Notes on the state of Virginia [1787]. Ed. by William Peden. Chapel Hill, N. C., 1955. 315 p.

"Articles agreed on & concluded at James Cittie in Virginia [1651]," p. 114-16. "An act of indempnitie made att the surrender of the countrey [1651]," p. 116-17.

JESTER, ANNIE L. AND MARTHA W. HIDEN, eds. Adventurers of purse and person. Virginia, 1607-1625. [n.p.] 1956. 442 p.

KINGSBURY, SUSAN M. A comparison of the Virginia company with the other English trading companies of the 16th and 17th centuries. Am. hist. assoc., Report, 1906, v. 1, p. 159-76.

LEFROY, SIR JOHN H. Memorials of the discovery and early settlement of the Bermudas or Somers islands, 1516-1685. London, 1877-1879. 2 v.

MASON, GEORGE C. The case against Henricopolis. Va. mag., 56 (1948), 350-53.

MOOK, MAURICE A. The ethnological significance of Tindall's map of Virginia, 1608. W & M quar. (ser. 2), 23 (1943), 371-408.

____Virginia ethnology from an early relation [an analysis of Archer's "A relatyon of the discovery of our river"] W & M quar. (ser. 2), 23 (1943), 101-29.

MORISON, SAMUEL E. The Plymouth colony and Virginia. Va. mag., 62 (1954), 147-65.

MORTON, RICHARD L. Struggle against tyranny and the beginning of a new era, 1677-1699. Williamsburg, 1957. (Jamestown 350th anniversary historical booklet, No. 9.)

NEILL, EDWARD D. Early settlement of Virginia and Virginiola, as noticed by poets and players in the time of Shakspeare, with some letters on the colonization of America, never before printed. Minneapolis, Minn., 1878. 47 p.

14

_____The English colonization of America during the seventeenth century. London, 1871. 352 p.

_____English maids for Virginia planters. Ships arriving at Jamestown, from the settlement of Virginia until the revocation of charter of London company. New England hist. and gen. register, 30 (1876), 410-12, 414-18.

_____History of the Virginia company of London. Albany, N. Y., 1869. 432 p.

_____Virginia, as a penal colony. Historical mag. (ser. 2), 5 (1869), 296-97.

_____Virginia Carolorum: the colony under the rule of Charles the First and Second . . . 1625-1685. Albany, N. Y., 1886. 446 p.

_____Virginia company of London. Extracts from their manuscript transactions. Washington, 1868. 17 p.

_____Virginia governors under the London company. Saint Paul, Minn., 1889. 35 p.

_____The Virginia lotteries. Virginia slaveholders, Feb., 1625. New England hist. and gen. register, 31 (1877), 21-22.

_____Virginia vetusta, during the reign of James the First. Albany, N. Y., 1885. 216 p.

PHILLIPS, PHILIP L. Some early maps of Virginia and the makers, including plates relating to the first settlement of Jamestown. Va. mag., 15 (1907), 71-81.

SAINSBURY, W. NOEL. The first settlement of French protestants in America [1634]. Antiquary, 3 (1881), 101-3.

SAMS, CONWAY W. The conquest of Virginia: the second attempt . . . 1606-1610. Norfolk, Va., 1929. 916 p.

15

_____The conquest of Virginia; the third attempt, 1610-1624. N. Y., 1939. 824 p.

STANARD, MARY N. The story of Virginia's first century. Philadelphia, 1928. 331 p.

STANARD, WILLIAM G. Some emigrants to Virginia. Memoranda in regard to several hundred emigrants to Virginia during the colonial period. Richmond, 1911. 79 p.

STEPHENSON, N. W. Some inner history of the Virginia company. W & M quar. (ser. 1), 22 (1913), 89-98.

SWEM, EARL G., ed. Jamestown 350th anniversary historical booklets. Williamsburg, 1957. 23 v.

> Contents: 1) E. G. Swem, J. M. Jennings and J. A. Servies, A selected bibliography of Virginia, 1607-1699. 2) W. W. Abbot, A Virginia chronology, 1585-1783. 3) B. C. McCary, Captain John Smith's map of Virginia. 4) S. M. Bemiss, The three charters of the Virginia company of London. 5) W. F. Craven, The Virginia company of London, 1606-1624. 6) C. E. Hatch, The first seventeen years at Jamestown, 1607-1624. 7) W. E. Washburn, Virginia under Charles I, and Cromwell, 1625-1660. 8) T. J. Wertenbaker, Bacon's rebellion, 1676. 9) R. L. Morton, Struggle against tyranny and the beginning of a new era, 1677-1699. 10) G. M. Brydon, The faith of our fathers; religion in Virginia, 1607-1699. 11) H. C. Forman, Virginia architecture in seventeenth century. 12) W. S. Robinson, Mother earth; land grants in Virginia, 1607-1699. 13) James Wharton, The bounty of the Chesapeake; fishing in colonial Virginia, 1607-1699. 14) Lyman Carrier, Agriculture in Virginia, 1607-1699. 15) S. M. Ames, Reading, writing and arithmetic in Virginia, 1607-1699. 16) T. J. Wertenbaker, The government of Virginia in the seventeenth century. 17) A. L. Jester, Domestic life in Virginia, 1607-1699. 18) B. C. McCary, Indians in seventeenth century Virginia. 19) M. W. Hiden, How justice grew; the counties of Virginia; an abstract of their formation. 20) Melvin Herndon, The sovereign remedy; tobacco in colonial Virginia. 21) T. P. Hughes, Medicine in Virginia, 1607-1699. 22) C. W. Evans, Some notes on shipping and shipbuilding in colonial Virginia. 23) J. P. Hudson, Jamestown commodities in the seventeenth century.

[T., J. W.] THE RECORDS OF the London company for the first colony in Virginia. Historical magazine, 2 (1858), 33-35.

TORRENCE, WILLIAM C., comp. Virginia wills and administrations, 1632-1800. Richmond [1931] 483 p.

TRAYLOR, ROBERT L. Some notes on the first recorded visit of white men to the site of the present city of Richmond, Virginia. Richmond, 1899. 20 p.

TYLER, LYON G. England in America, 1580-1652. N. Y., 1904. 355 p.

——London company records. Am. hist. assoc., Repoıt (1901), v. 1, p. 543-550.

WASHBURN, WILCOMB E. Virginia under Charles I, and Cromwell, 1625-1660. Williamsburg, 1957. (Jamestown 350th anniversary historical booklet, No. 7.)

WATERMAN, THOMAS T. Domestic colonial architecture of Tidewater Virginia. N. Y., 1932. 191 p.

WERTENBAKER, THOMAS J. The government of Virginia in the seventeenth century. Williamsburg, 1957. (Jamestown 350th anniversary historical booklet, No. 16.)

——Virginia under the Stuarts, 1607-1688. Princeton, N. J., 1914. 271 p.

WISE, JENNINGS C. Ye kingdome of Accowmacke; or, The Eastern Shore of Virginia in the seventeenth century. Richmond, 1911. 406 p.

WRIGHT, LOUIS B. The first gentlemen of Virginia. San Marino, Calif., 1940. 373 p.

YARDLEY, JOHN H. R. Before the Mayflower. N. Y., 1931. 408 p.

JAMESTOWN

CAYWOOD, LOUIS R. Excavations at Green Spring plantation. Yorktown, Va., 1955. 29 p.

COTTER, JOHN L. AND J. P. HUDSON. New discoveries at Jamestown. Washington, 1957. 99 p.

FORMAN, HENRY C. The bygone "Subberbs of James Cittie." W & M quar. (ser. 2), 20 (1940), 475-86.

_____Jamestown and St. Mary's, buried cities of romance. Baltimore, 1938. 355 p.

GOOKIN, WARNER F. The first leaders at Jamestown [1606-1607]. Va. mag., 58 (1950), 181-93.

GREGORY, GEORGE C. Jamestown first brick state house. Va. mag., 43 (1935), 193-99.

HATCH, CHARLES E. The first seventeen years at Jamestown, 1607-1624. Williamsburg, 1957. (Jamestown 350th anniversary historical booklet, No. 6.)

_____Jamestown, Virginia; the town site and its story. [Washington, 1957] 54 p.

RILEY, EDWARD M. and CHARLES E. HATCH, eds. James Towne in the words of contemporaries. Washington, 1955. 36 p.

TYLER, LYON G. The cradle of the republic: Jamestown and James River. [2nd ed.] Richmond, 1906. 286 p.

YONGE, SAMUEL H. The site of old "James Towne," 1607-1698. Richmond, 1907. 151 p.

AMES, SUSIE M. Reading, writing and arithmetic in Virginia, 1607-1699. Williamsburg, 1957. (Jamestown 350th anniversary historical booklet, No. 15.)

[ARMSTRONG, MRS. F. M.] The Syms-Eaton free school. Benjamin Syms, 1634; Thomas Eaton, 1659. [n.p., n.d.] 26 p.

BLANTON, WYNDHAM B. Medicine in Virginia in the seventeenth century. Richmond [1930] 337 p.

BRUCE, PHILIP A. Institutional history of Virginia in the seventeenth century; an inquiry into the religious, moral, educational, legal, military, and political condition of the people. N. Y., 1910. 2 v.

_____Social life of Virginia in the seventeenth century. An inquiry into the origin of the higher planting class, together with an account of the habits, customs, and diversions of the people. 2nd. ed. Lynchburg, Va., 1927. 275 p.

BUCK, JAMES L. B. The development of public schools in Virginia, 1607-1952. Richmond [1952] 572 p. (Va. State board of educ., Bulletin, v. 35, no. 1)

CAMPBELL, HELEN J. The Syms and Eaton Schools and their successors. W & M Quar. (series 2), 20 (1940), 1-61.

COMENIUS IN ENGLAND; the visit of Jan Amos Komensky (Comenius), the Czech philosopher and educationalist, to London, in 1641-1642; its bearing on the origins of the Royal society, on the development of the encyclopedia, and on plans for the higher education of the Indians of New England and Virginia. Ed. by Robert F. Young. London, 1932. 99 p.

CROZIER, WILLIAM A. Virginia colonial militia, 1651-1776. N. Y., 1905. 144 p.

HUGHES, THOMAS P. Medicine in Virginia, 1607-1699. Williamsburg, 1957. (Jamestown 350th anniversary historical booklet, No. 21.)

JESTER, ANNIE L. Domestic life in Virginia, 1607-1699. Williamsburg, 1957. (Jamestown 350th anniversary historical booklet, No. 17.)

LAND, ROBERT H. Henrico and its college. W & M quar. (ser. 2), 18 (1938), 453-98.

McCABE, W. GORDON. The first university in America, 1619-1622. Va. mag., 30 (1922), 133-56.

McMURTRIE, DOUGLAS C. The first printing in Virginia; the abortive attempt at Jamestown, the first permanent press at Williamsburg, the early gazettes, and the work of other Virginia typographic pioneers. Vienna, 1935. 15 p.

NEILL, EDWARD D. History of education in Virginia during the seventeenth century. Washington, 1867. 27 p.

____A study of the Virginia census of 1624. New England hist. and gen. register, 31 (1877), 147-53, 265-72, 393-401.

POWELL, WILLIAM S. Books in the Virginia colony before 1624. W & M quar. (ser. 3), 5 (1948), 177-84.

SHURTLEFF, HAROLD R. The log cabin myth; a study of the early dwellings of the English colonists in North America. Cambridge, Mass., 1939. 243 p.

SMART, G. K. Private libraries in colonial Virginia. Am. literature, 10 (1938), 24-52.

TYLER, LYON G. The College of William and Mary in Virginia: its history and work, 1693-1907. Richmond, 1907. 96 p.

WERTENBAKER, THOMAS J. Patrician and plebeian in Virginia. Charlottesville, Va., 1910. 239 p.

_____The planters of colonial Virginia. Princeton, N. J., 1922. 260 p.

ECONOMICS

ANDREWS, CHARLES M. British committees, commissions, and councils of trade and plantations, 1622-1675. Baltimore, 1908. 151 p. (Johns Hopkins univ. studies in hist. and pol. sci., ser. 26, nos. 1-3)

BALLAGH, JAMES C. White servitude in the colony of Virginia. Baltimore, 1895. 99 p. (Johns Hopkins univ. studies in hist. and pol. sci., ser. 13, nos. 6-7)

BARNES, VIOLA F. Land tenure in the English colonial charters of the seventeenth century. In: Essays in colonial history presented to Charles M. Andrews, New Haven, Conn., 1931, p. 4-40.

BASSETT, JOHN S. The relation between the Virginia planter and the London merchant. Am. hist. assoc., Report (1901), v. 1, p. 551-75.

BRUCE, KATHLEEN. Virginia iron manufacture in the slave era. N. Y., 1930. 482 p.

BRUCE, PHILIP A. Economic history of Virginia in the seventeenth century. N. Y., 1895. 2 v.

EVANS, CERINDA W. Some notes on shipping and shipbuilding in colonial Virginia. Williamsburg, 1957. (Jamestown 350th anniversary historical booklet, No. 22.)

HANDLIN, OSCAR, AND MARY HANDLIN. Origins of the southern labor system [1607-1705] W & M quar. (ser. 3), 7 (1950), 199-222.

HARRINGTON, JEAN C. Glassmaking at Jamestown, America's first industry. Richmond [1952] 47 p.

21

HARRISON, FAIRFAX. Virginia land grants: a study of conveyancing in relation to colonial politics. Richmond, 1925. 184 p.

HATCH, CHARLES E. Glassmaking in Virginia, 1607-1625. W & M quar. (ser. 2), 21 (1941), 119-38, 227-38.

HUDSON, J. P. Jamestown commodities in the seventeenth century. Williamsburg, 1957. (Jamestown 350th anniversary historical booklet, No. 23.)

JUDAH, CHARLES B. The North American fisheries and British policy to 1713. Urbana, Ill., 1933. 183 p.

MACPHERSON, DAVID. Annals of commerce, manufactures, fisheries, and navigation. London, 1805. 4 v.

READ, THOMAS T. Gold and the Virginia colony. Columbia university quarterly, 26 (1934), 43-47.

RIPLEY, WILLIAM Z. The financial history of Virginia, 1609-1776. N. Y., 1893. 170 p. (Columbia univ. studies in hist., econ., and pub. law, v. 4, no. 1)

ROBINSON, W. STITT. Mother earth; land grants in Virginia, 1607-1699. Williamsburg, 1957. (Jamestown 350th anniversary historical booklet, No. 12.)

SMITH, ABBOT E. Colonists in bondage: white servitude and convict labor in America. 1607-1776. Chapel Hill, N. C., 1947. 435 p.

WHARTON, JAMES. The bounty of the Chesapeake; fishing in colonial Virginia, 1607-1699. Williamsburg, 1957. (Jamestown 350th anniversary historical booklet, No. 13.)

WILLIAMS, LLOYD H. Pirates of colonial Virginia. Richmond, 1937. 139 p.

LAW AND POLITICS

ALLEN, JOHN W. English political thought, 1603-1660 (v. 1, 1603-1644). London, 1938. 525 p.

AMES, SUSIE M. The reunion of two Virginia counties. Journal of Southern history, 8 (1942), 536-48.

BIRCH, THOMAS. The court and times of James the First. London, 1849. 2 v.

BROWN, ALEXANDER. English politics in early Virginia history. Boston, 1901. 277 p.

CHANDLER, JULIAN A. C. The history of suffrage in Virginia. Baltimore, 1901. 76 p. (Johns Hopkins univ. studies in hist. and pol. sci., ser. 19, no. 6-7)

CHITWOOD, OLIVER P. Justice in colonial Virginia. Baltimore, 1905. 123 p. (Johns Hopkins univ. studies in hist. and pol. sci., ser. 23, no. 7-8)

CHUMBLEY, GEORGE L. Colonial justice in Virginia; the development of a judicial system, typical laws and cases of the period. Richmond, 1938. 174 p.

CRUMP, HELEN J. Colonial admiralty jurisdiction in the seventeenth century. London, 1931. 200 p.

FLIPPIN, PERCY S. Financial administration of the colony of Virginia. Baltimore, 1915. 95 p. (Johns Hopkins univ. studies in hist. and pol. sci., ser. 33, no. 2)

_____The royal government in Virginia, 1624-1775. N. Y., 1919. 393 p. (Columbia univ. stud. in hist., econ., and pub. law, v. 84, no. 1)

FULLER, HUGH N. [and others] Criminal justice in Virginia. N. Y., 1931. 195 p.

GORDON, ARMISTEAD C. The laws of Bacon's assembly. [Charlottesville, Va., 1914] 12 p.

HANNAY, DAVID. The great chartered companies. London, 1926. 258 p.

HARPER, LAWRENCE A. The English navigation laws: a seventeenth-century experiment in social engineering. N. Y., 1939. 503 p.

HATCH, CHARLES E. The oldest legislative assembly in America & its first state house. [Rev. ed.] Washington, 1947. 30 p.

HENRY, WILLIAM W. The first legislative assembly in America. Am. hist. assoc., Report, 1893, p. 297-316.

HIDEN, MARTHA W. How justice grew; the counties of Virginia: an abstract of their formation. Williamsburg, 1957. (Jamestown 350th anniversary historical booklet, No. 19.)

KARRAKER, CYRUS H. The seventeenth-century sheriff; a comparative study of the sheriff in England and the Chesapeake colonies, 1607-1689. Chapel Hill, N. C., 1930. 219 p.

LATANÉ, JOHN H. The early relations between Maryland and Virginia. Baltimore, 1895. 81 p. (Johns Hopkins univ. stud. in hist. and pol. sci., ser. 13, no. 3-4)

NEILL, EDWARD D. The earliest contest in America on charter-rights, begun A.D. 1619, in Virginia legislature. Macalester college, Contributions (ser. 1), 5 (1890), 141-68.

PORTER, ALBERT O. County government in Virginia, a legislative history, 1607-1904. N. Y., 1947. 356 p.

PRINCE, WALTER F. The first criminal code of Virginia. Am hist. assoc., Report (1899), v. 1, p. 309-363.

SCOTT, ARTHUR P. Criminal law in colonial Virginia. Chicago, 1930. 335 p.

AGRICULTURE

ARENTS, GEORGE. The seed from which Virginia grew. W & M quar. (ser. 2), 19 (1939), 123-29.

_____Tobacco; its history illustrated by the books, manuscripts and engravings in the library of George Arents, Jr.; bibliographic notes by Jerome E. Brooks. N. Y., 1937-1952. 5 v.

CABELL, NATHANIEL F. Early history of agriculture in Virginia. Washington [n.d.] 41 p.

CARRIER, LYMAN. Agriculture in Virginia, 1607-1699. Williamsburg, 1957. (Jamestown 350th anniversary historical booklet, No. 14.)

CRAVEN, AVERY O. Soil exhaustion as a factor in the agricultural history of Virginia and Maryland, 1606-1860. Urbana, Ill., 1926. 179 p.

GRAY, LEWIS C. History of agriculture in the southern United States to 1860. Washington, 1933. 2 v. (Carnegie institution publication, no. 430)

HERNDON, MELVIN. The sovereign remedy; tobacco in colonial Virginia. Williamsburg, 1957. (Jamestown 350th anniversary historical booklet, No. 20.)

ROBERT, JOSEPH C. The story of tobacco in America. N. Y., 1949. 296 p.

TATHAM, WILLIAM. An historical and practical essay on the culture and commerce of tobacco. London, 1800. 330 p.

INDIANS

BUSHNELL, DAVID I. The five Monacan towns in Virginia, 1607. Washington, 1930. 38 p.

_____Indian sites below the falls of the Rappahannock, Virginia. Washington, 1937. 65 p. (Smithsonian misc. collections, v. 96, no. 4)

_____The Monahoac tribes in Virginia, 1608. Washington, 1935. 56 p. (Smithsonian misc. collections, v. 94, no. 8)

____Virginia—from early records. Am. anthropologist (new ser.)
9 (1907), 31-44.

McCary, Ben C. Indians in seventeenth-century Virginia. Wil
liamsburg, 1957. (Jamestown 350th anniversary historica]
booklet, No. 18.)

Mooney, James. The Powhatan confederacy, past and present.
Am. anthropologist (new ser.), 9 (1907), 129-152.

Morrison, Alfred J. The Virginia Indian trade to 1673. W &
M quar. (ser. 2), 1 (1921), 217-36.

Neill, Edward D. Massacre at Falling Creek, Virginia, March
22, 1621/22. Magazine of Am. hist., 1 (1877), 222-25.

Robinson, W. Stitt. Indian education and missions in colonial
Virginia. Journal of Southern history, 18 (1952), 152-68.

Willoughby, Charles C. The Virginia Indians in the seventeenth century. Am. anthropologist, 9 (1907), 57-86.

BACON'S REBELLION, 1676

Bayne, Howard R. A rebellion in the colony of Virginia. [N. Y.,
1904] 16 p. (Society of colonial wars in the state of N. Y.,
Historical papers, no. 7)

Brent, Frank P. Some unpublished facts relating to Bacon's
rebellion on the Eastern Shore of Virginia, gleaned from the
court records of Accomac county. Va. hist. soc., Collections
(new ser.), 11 (1892), 177-89.

Lane, John H. The birth of liberty; a story of Bacon's rebellion.
Richmond, 1909. 181 p.

Stanard, Mary N. The story of Bacon's rebellion. N. Y., 1907.
181 p.

26

STEARNS, BERTHA M. The literary treatment of Bacon's rebellion in Virginia. Va. mag, 52 (1944), 163-179.

WARE, WILLIAM. A memoir of Nathaniel Bacon. In: Jared Sparks, Library of American biography, Boston, 1844, ser. 2, v. 3, p. 239-306.

WERTENBAKER, THOMAS J. Bacon's rebellion, 1676. Williamsburg, 1957. (Jamestown 350th anniversary historical booklet, No. 8.)

_____Torchbearer of the revolution, the story of Bacon's rebellion and its leader. Princeton, N. J., 1940. 237 p.

RELIGION

ANDERSON, JAMES S. M. The history of the Church of England in the colonies and foreign dependencies of the British empire. 2nd ed. London, 1856. 3 v.

BRYDON, GEORGE M. The faith of our fathers; religion in Virginia, 1607-1699. Williamsburg, 1957. (Jamestown 350th anniversary historical booklet, No. 10.)

_____Virginia's mother church and the political conditions under which it grew. Richmond, 1947-52. 2 v.

COLONIAL CHURCHES; a series of sketches of churches in the original colony of Virginia. Richmond, 1907. 319 p.

CROSS, ARTHUR L. The Anglican Episcopate and the American colonies. N. Y., 1902. 368 p.

EDMUNDSON, WILLIAM. A journal of the life, travels, sufferings and labour of love in the work of the ministry. 2nd ed. London, 1774. 371 p.
  Description of Virginia in 1672, p. 66-72.

GOODWIN, EDWARD L. The colonial church in Virginia. Milwaukee. Wis. [1927] 342 p.

27

GOODWIN, WILLIAM A. R. The records of Bruton parish church; ed. by Mary Frances Goodwin. Richmond, 1941. 205 p.

HAWKINS, ERNEST. Historical notices of the missions of the Church of England in the North American colonies, previous to the independence of the United States. London, 1845. 447 p.

[HAWKS, FRANCIS L.] A narrative of events connected with the rise and progress of the Protestant Episcopal church in Virginia. To which is added ... the Journals of the conventions in Virginia from the commencement to the present time. N. Y., 1836. 286, 332 p.

LITTLE, LEWIS P. Imprisoned preachers and religious liberty in Virginia. Lynchburg, Va., 1938. 534 p.

MCILWAINE, HENRY R. The struggle of protestant dissenters for religious toleration in Virginia. Baltimore, 1894. 67 p. (Johns Hopkins univ. stud. in hist. and pol. sci., ser. 12, no. 4)

MASON, GEORGE C. Colonial churches of Tidewater Virginia. Richmond, 1945. 381 p.

MILLER, PERRY. Religion and society in the early literature: the religious impulse in the founding of Virginia [1619-1624]. W & M quar. (ser. 3), 6 (1949), 24-41.

____The religious impulse in the founding of Virginia: religion and society in the early literature [1606-1622]. W & M quar. (ser. 3), 5 (1948), 492-522.

PENNINGTON, EDGAR L. The Church of England in colonial Virginia; pt. 1, 1607-1619. Hartford, Conn., 1937. 22 p.

PERRY, WILLIAM S. Historical collections relating to the American colonial church. v. 1, Virginia. [Hartford, Conn.] 1870. 585 p.

_____The history of the American Episcopal church, 1587-1883. Boston, 1885. 2 v.

Seiler, William H. The Church of England as the established church in seventeenth-century Virginia [1606-1705] Journal of southern history, 15 (1949), 478-508.

Thomas, R. S. The old brick church, near Smithfield, Virginia. Built in 1632. Va. hist. soc., Collections (new ser.), 11 (1892), 127-63.

_____The religious element in the settlement at Jamestown in 1607. Petersburg, Va., 1898. 36 p.

The Negro

Ballagh, James C. A history of slavery in Virginia. Baltimore, 1902. 160 p. (Johns Hopkins univ. studies in hist. and pol. sci., extra vol., 24)

Phillips, Ulrich B. American Negro slavery. N. Y., 1918. 529 p.

Russell, John H. The free Negro in Virginia, 1619-1865. Baltimore, 1913. 194 p. (Johns Hopkins univ. studies in hist. and pol. science, ser. 31, no. 3)

Writers' program. Virginia. The Negro in Virginia. N. Y., 1940. 380 p.

Biography

Adams, Henry. Captain John Smith. North American Review, 104 (1867), 1-30.

Baxter, James P. Memoir of Sir Ferdinando Gorges. In: Sir Ferdinando Gorges and his province of Maine, Boston, 1890, v. 1, p. 1-198. (Prince society publications, no. 18)

BODDIE, JOHN B. Edward Bennett of London and Virginia. W & M quar. (ser. 2), 13 (1933), 117-30.

BURNYEAT, JOHN. John Burnyeat, 1665-1673 [a missionary in the American colonies]. Va. mag., 19 (1911), 58-60.

CHATTERTON, EDWARD K. Captain John Smith. N. Y., 1927. 286 p.

CLAIBORNE, JOHN H. William Claiborne of Virginia. N. Y., 1917. 231 p.

DAVIS, RICHARD B. George Sandys, poet-adventurer; a study in Anglo-American culture in the seventeenth century. N .Y., 1955. 320 p.

EDWARDS, EDWARD. The life of Sir Walter Raleigh. Based on contemporary documents . . . together with his letters now first collected. [London] 1868. 2 v.

FLETCHER, JOHN G. John Smith—also Pocahontas. N. Y., [1928] 303 p.

GLENN, KEITH. Captain John Smith and the Indians. Va. mag., 52 (1944), 228-48.

HALE, NATHANIEL C. Virginia venturer, a historical biography of William Claiborne, 1600-1677; the story of the merchant venturers who founded Virginia, and the war in the Chesapeake. Richmond [1951] 340 p.

HARLOW, VINCENT T. ed. The voyages of Captain William Jackson (1642-1645). London, 1923. 39 p.

HARRISON, FAIRFAX. Henry Norwood (1615-1689), treasurer of Virginia, 1661-1673. Va. mag., 33 (1925), 1-10.

HECK, EARL L. W. Augustine Herrman, beginner of the Virginia tobacco trade. [Richmond] 1941. 123 p.

HENRY, WILLIAM W. The rescue of Captain John Smith by Pocahontas. Potters American monthly, 4 (1875), 523-28; 5 (1875), 591-97.

HERNDON, JOHN G. The Reverend William Wilkinson of England, Virginia, and Maryland [1612?-1663]. Va. mag., 57 (1949), 316-321.

LEE, CAZENOVE G. JR., Lee Chronicle, a history of the Lees of Virginia. N. Y., 1956. 315 p.

LEE, EDMUND J. Lee of Virginia, 1642-1892. Philadelphia [1895] 586 p.

MORSE, JARVIS M. John Smith and his critics. Journal of Southern history, 1 (1935), 124-37.

MOTLEY, DANIEL E. Life of Commissary James Blair, founder of William and Mary college. Baltimore, 1901. 57 p. (Johns Hopkins univ. studies in hist. and pol. science, ser. 19, no. 10)

NEILL, EDWARD D. Captain John Smith, adventurer and romancer. Macalester college, Contributions (ser. 1), 11 (1890), 241-51.

_____Memoir of Rev. Patrick Copland, rector elect of the first projected college in the United States. N. Y., 1871. 96 p.

_____Pocahontas and her companions; a chapter from the history of the Virginia company of London. Albany, N. Y., 1869. 32 p.

PECKARD, PETER. Memoirs of the life of Mr. Nicholas Ferrar. Cambridge, 1790. 316 p.

PENNINGTON, EDGAR L. Commissary Blair. Hartford, Conn., 1936. 24 p.

31

POINDEXTER, CHARLES. Captain John Smith and his critics. Richmond, 1893. 74 p.

PRING, JAMES H. Captaine Martin Pringe, the last of the Elizabethan seamen. Plymouth [Eng.], 1888. 34 p.

ROBERTSON, WYNDHAM. Pocahontas, alias Matoaka, and her descendants . . . historical notes by R. A. Brock. Richmond, 1887. 84 p.

SHEPPARD, WILLIAM L. The Princess Pocahontas; her story. From the original authorities. Richmond, 1907. 17 p.

SHIRLEY, JOHN W. George Percy at Jamestown, 1607-1612. Va. Mag., 57 (1949), 227-43.

SMITH, BRADFORD. John Smith, his life and legend. Philadelphia, 1953. 375 p.

SMYTH, CLIFFORD. Captain John Smith and England's first successful colony in America. N. Y., 1931. 176 p.

SOUTHALL, JAMES P. C. Captain John Martin of Brandon on the James. Va. Mag., 54 (1946), p. 21-67.

STEWART, ROBERT A. The first William Byrd of Charles City county, Virginia. Va. mag., 41 (1933), 189-95, 323-29.

SYME, RONALD. John Smith of Virginia. N. Y., 1954. 192 p.

WEBSTER, MRS. M. M. Pocahontas. A legend, with historical and traditionary notes. Philadelphia, 1840. 220 p.

FICTION AND DRAMA

BEHN, APHRA. The widdow ranter, or The history of Bacon in Virginia. A tragi-comedy. London, 1690. 56 p.

BENET, STEPHEN VINCENT. Western star. N. Y. [1943]. 181 p.

Cooke, John E. My lady Pokahontas. A true relation of Virginia. Writ by Anas Todkill, puritan and pilgrim. Boston, 1885. 190 p.

[Davis, John] Captain Smith and Princess Pocahontas, an Indian tale. Philadelphia, 1817. 90 p.

_____The first settlers of Virginia, an historical novel. 2nd ed. N. Y., 1806. 284 p.

Freeman, Mary E. W. The heart's highway; a romance of Virginia in the seventeenth-century. N. Y., 1900. 308 p.

Goodwin, Mrs. Maud (Wilder). The head of a hundred, being an account of certain passages in the life of Humphrey Huntoon, sometime an officer in the colony of Virginia. Boston, 1895. 225 p.

_____White aprons; a romance of Bacon's rebellion, Virginia, 1676. Boston, 1896. 339 p.

Johnston, Mary. Prisoners of hope; a tale of colonial Virginia. Boston, 1898. 378 p.

_____To have and to hold. Boston, 1900. 403 p.

Tucker, Henry St. G. Hansford; a tale of Bacon's rebellion. Richmond, 1857. 356 p.

PRIMARY WORKS

COLLECTIONS

ANDREWS, CHARLES M., ed. Narratives of the insurrections, 1675-1690. N. Y., 1915. 414 p.

THE ASPINWALL PAPERS. Virginia [1617-1676]. Mass. hist. soc., Collections (ser. 4), 9 (1871), 1-187.

> John Harvey, A brief declaration of the state of Virginia, 1624, p. 60-81; Thomas Yong, Voyage to Virginia and Delaware Bay and river in 1634, p. 81-131; Virginias deploured condition, 1676, p. 162-76.

BEMISS, SAMUEL M. The three charters of the Virginia company of London and seven related documents. Williamsburg, 1957. (Jamestown 350th anniversary historical booklet, No. 4.)

BRIGHAM, CLARENCE S., ed. British royal proclamations relating to America, 1603-1783. Worcester, Mass., 1911. 268 p. (Am. antiq. soc. Transactions, v. 12)

BROCK, ROBERT A. Documents, chiefly unpublished, relating to the Huguenot emigration to Virginia. Richmond, 1886. 247 p. (Va. hist. soc., Collections, n.s., v. 5)

BROWN UNIVERSITY. John Carter Brown library. Three proclamations concerning the lottery for Virginia, 1613-1621. Providence, R. I., 1907. 3, 4 p.

> Contents: [1] By his Majesties councell for Virginia, 1613. [2] A declaration for the certaine time of drawing the great standing lottery, 1615. [3] By the King [a proclamation], 1620.

CATTERALL, HELEN T., ed. Judicial cases concerning American slavery and the Negro. Washington, 1926-37. 5 v. (Carnegie inst., Publication no. 374)

> v. 1: "Cases from the courts of England, Virginia, West Virginia, and Kentucky."

COLONIAL RECORDS of Virginia. Richmond, 1874. 106 p.

Contents: 1) The first assembly of Virginia, held July 30, 1619. 2) List of the livinge and the dead in Virginia, Feb. 16, 1623. 3) A briefe declaration of the plantation of Virginia, during the first twelve years. 4) A list of the number of men, women and children, inhabitants in the several counties within the collony of Virginia, in 1634. 5) A letter from Charles II, acknowledging the receipt of a present of Virginia silk, 1668. 6.) A list of the parishes in Virginia, 1680.

COPLAND, PATRICK. Letters of Patrick Copland [1623, 1646]. W & M quar. (ser. 2), 9 (1929), 300-302.

DONNAN, ELIZABETH, ed. Documents illustrative of the history of the slave trade to America. Washington, 1930-1935. 4 v.

v. 1, "1441-1700." v. 2, "Southern colonies."

FITZHUGH, WILLIAM. Letters of William Fitzhugh [1679-1699]. Va. mag., 1 (1893), 17-55; continued to 6 (1898).

FLEET, BEVERLEY AND L. O. DUVALL, comps. Virginia colonial abstracts. v. 1-34; ser. 2, v. 1- Richmond, 1937(?)-date.

Titles touching the seventeenth century follow:

_____Acchawmacke, 1632-1637. Richmond [1943] 111 p. (Virginia colonial abstracts, v. 18)

_____Accomacke county, 1637-1640. Richmond [1948] 103 p. (Virginia colonial abstracts, v. 32)

_____Charles City county court orders, 1655-58. Richmond [1941-42] 4 v. (Virginia colonial abstracts, v. 10-13)

_____Huntington library data, 1607-1850. Richmond [1947] 109 p. (Virginia colonial abstracts, v. 30)

_____Lancaster county [court records] 1652-1655. Richmond [1944] 110 p. (Virginia colonial abstracts, v. 22)

_____Lancaster county, record book 2. 1654-1666, pages 1-394. Richmond [n.d.] 137 p. (Virginia colonial abstracts, v. 1)

_____Lower Norfolk county, 1651-1654. Richmond [1948] 106 p. (Virginia colonial abstracts, v. 31)

35

_____Northumberland co. Record of births, 1661-1810. Richmond [1938] 134 p. (Virginia colonial abstracts, v. 3)

_____Northumberland county records. 1652-1655. Richmond [1937?] 141 p. (Virginia colonial abstracts, v. 2)

_____Northumbria collectanea, 1645-1720. Richmond [1943-44] 2 v. (Virginia colonial abstracts, v. 19-20)

_____Richmond county records, 1692-1724. Richmond [1942-43] 2 v. (Virginia colonial abstracts, v. 16-17)

_____Virginia company of London, 1607-1624; ed. by Lindsay O. Duvall. [n.p., 1955] 121 p. (Virginia colonial abstracts, ser. 2, v. 3)

_____Westmoreland county, 1653-1657. Richmond [1945] 102 p. (Virginia colonial abstracts, v. 23)

_____York county, 1633-1657. Richmond [1945-46] 3 v. (Virginia colonial abstracts, v. 24-26)

FORCE, PETER, comp. Tracts and other papers, relating principally to the origin, settlement, and progress of the colonies in North America, from the discovery of the country to the year 1776. Washington, 1836-46. 4 v.

Vol. 1, no. 6, [Robert Johnson] Nova Britannia, 1609; no. 7 [Robert Johnson] The new life of Virginea, 1612; no. 8, [Thomas Mathew] The beginning, progress, and conclusion of Bacon's rebellion; no. 9, Mrs. Anne Cotton, An account of our late troubles in Virginia; no. 10, Sir William Berkeley, A list of those that have been executed for the late rebellion; no. 11, A narrative of the Indian and civil wars in Virginia.

Vol. 2, no. 6, Extract from a manuscript collection of annals relative to Virginia, 1642; no. 7, A description of the province of New Albion, 1648; no. 8, A perfect description of Virginia, 1649; no. 9, Virginia and Maryland, or, The Lord Baltamore's printed case, 1655.

Vol. 3, no. 1, [Virginia company of London] A true declaration of the estate of the colonie in Virginia, 1610; no. 2, [William Strachey, ed.] For the colony in Virginea Britannia. Lawes divine, morall and martiall, &c., 1612; no. 5, Virginia company of London, A declaration of the state of the colonie, 1620; no. 6, Virginia company of London, Orders and constitutions, 1619-1620; no. 7, Nathaniel Shrigley, A true relation of Virginia and Maryland, 1669; no. 10, [Henry Norwood] A voyage to

Virginia, 1649; no. 11, [Edward Williams] Virginia, more especially the south part thereof, richly and truly valued, 1650; no. 12, John Clayton, Letter . . . to the Royal society, 1688; no. 13 [Samuel Hartlib] The reformed Virginian silk-worm, 1655; no. 14, John Hammond, Leah and Rachel, or, The two fruitful sisters Virginia, and Maryland; no. 15, [Robert Greene] Virginia's cure, or, An advisive narrative concerning Virginia, 1662.

Vol. 1, no. 1-13; v. 2, no. 1-4, 6-7 reprinted: American colonial tracts monthly, v. 1, no. 1-12, v. 2, no. 1-6, Rochester, N. Y., 1897-98.

GREAT BRITAIN. Privy Council. Acts of the Privy council of England, colonial series, v. 1, A.D. 1613-1680. London, 1908. 930 p.

_____Public Record Office. Calendar of state papers, colonial series, America and West Indies [1574-1699] London, 1860-1908. 10 v.

HAKLUYT, RICHARD. The principal navigations, voyages, traffiques, and discoveries of the English nation. Ed. by Edmund Goldsmid. Edinburgh, 1885-1890. 16 v.

HALE, EDWARD E., ed. Original documents . . . illustrating the history of Sir Walter Raleigh's first American colony, and the colony at Jamestown. Am. antiq. soc., Transactions, 4 (1860), 1-65.

[Archer] A relatyon of the discovery of our river [1607], p. 40-65.

HALL, CLAYTON C., ed. Narratives of early Maryland, 1633-1684. N. Y., 1910. 460 p.

"The Lord Baltemore's case, 1653," p. 167-80; "Virginia and Maryland, or The Lord Baltemore's printed case uncased and answered, 1655," p. 187-230; "Leah and Rachel," by John Hammond, 1656, p. 281-308.

HAYWARD, NICHOLAS, Nicholas George, and Joseph Taylor. Old letters from Virginia county records [1652-1705]. W & M quar. (ser. 1), 11 (1903), 169-74.

HAZARD, EBENEZER. Historical collections; consisting of state papers, and other authentic documents. Philadelphia, 1792-94. 2 v.

"Articles agreed on and concluded at James Cittie in Virginia [1651]," v. 1, p. 560-61. "Articles for the surrendering of Virginia to the subjection of the parliament of the commonwealth of England [1651]," v. 1, p. 562-63. "An act of indempnitie made att the surrender of the countrey [1651]," v. 1, p. 563-64. [An act prohibiting trade with the Barbados, Antego, Bermudas, and Virginia, 1650] v. 1, p. 636-38.

HENING, WILLIAM W., ed. The statutes at large; being a collection of all the laws of Virginia . . . 1619 [through the session of 1792]. Richmond, 1809-1823. 13 v.

Indexed in E. G. Swem, Virginia historical index.

JENSEN, MERRILL, ed. English historical documents; American colonial documents to 1776. N. Y., 1955. 888 p. (English historical documents, v. 9)

KINGSBURY, SUSAN M., ed. The records of the Virginia company of London. Washington, 1906-1935. 4 v.

v. 1-2, "The court book" [April 28, 1619 to June 7, 1624]; v. 3-4, Documents, 1607-1626.

LABAREE, LEONARD W., ed. Royal instructions to British colonial governors, 1670-1776. N. Y., 1935. 2 v.

LETTERS OF THE Byrd family [to 1723]. Va. mag., 35 (1927), 221-45, 371-89.

[LIST OF TRACTS relating to Virginia in the library of Dorchester house, London, with a facsimile of a letter of Captain John Smith] Mass. hist. soc., Proceedings (ser. 2), 12 (1898), 158-61.

THE LOWER NORFOLK county, Virginia antiquary; ed. by Edward W. James. Baltimore, 1895-1906. 5 v.

Indexed in E. G. Swem, Virginia historical index.

LOWER NORFOLK county records, 1636-1646. Va. mag., 39 (1931), 1-20; continued to 41 (1933), 335-45.

MISCELLANEOUS COLONIAL documents [1672-73], from the originals in the Virginia state archives. Va. mag., 20 (1912), 22-32.

> Contents: Papers in regard to Capt. Thomas Gardner [1672-73]. Proceedings of Virginia council, Aug. 1673. Order in regard to fort, 1673. Proceedings of a court martial, Oct. 21, 1673.

NOTES FROM THE records of Stafford county, Virginia, order books [1692-93]. Va. mag., 47 (1939), 22-26, 126-32, 248-52, 335-48.

NUGENT, NELL M. Cavaliers and pioneers; abstracts of Virginia land patents and grants, 1623-1800. Vol. 1, 1623-1666 [all published] Richmond, 1934. 767 p.

PURCHAS, SAMUEL. Purchas his pilgrimes. In five bookes. London, 1625. 5 v.

> Reprinted as Hakluytus posthumous, or Purchas his pilgrimes. Glasgow, 1906. 20 v.

RANDOLPH, EDWARD. Edward Randolph; including his letters and official papers from the New England, middle, and southern colonies in America. Boston, 1898-1909. 7 v. (Prince society publications, v. 24-28, 30-31)

RANDOLPH MANUSCRIPT; Virginia seventeenth-century records. Va. mag., 15 (1908), 390-405, continued to 22 (1914), 337-47.

SACKVILLE, LIONEL C., 1st duke. Lord Sackville's papers respecting Virginia, 1613-1631. Am. hist. rev., 27 (1922), 493-538, 738-65.

SMITH, JOHN. Capt. John Smith, travels and works; ed. by Edward Arber. Edinburgh, 1910. 2 v.

> [Virginia company of London] Instructions by way of advice, for the intended voyage to Virginia [1606], v. 1, p. xxxiii-xxxvii. Tindall, Robert. Robert Tindall, gunner to Prince Henry. Letter to the prince, 22 June 1607, v. 1, p. xxxviii-xxxix.

[Archer, Gabriel] A relayton of the discovery . . . 21 May-22 June 1607, v. 1, p. xl-lv.
Percy, George. Observations gathered out of a discourse of the plantation of the southerne colonie in Virginia, 1606, v. 1, p. lvii-lxxiii.
Wingfield, Edward M. A discourse of Virginia, v. 1, p. lxxiv-xci.
Archer, Gabriel. Letter from JamesTown, 31 August 1609, v. 1, p. xciv-xcvii.
Ratcliffe, John. Letter to the Earl of Salisbury, 4 October 1609, v. 1, p. xcviii-xcix.
Spelman, Henry. Relation of Virginea, v. 1, p. ci-cxiv.
Smith, John. A true relation [1608], v. 1, p. 1-40.
A map of Virginia, 1612, v. 1, p. 41-174.
A description of New England, 1616, v. 1, p. 175-232.
The Generall historie of Virginia, 1624, v. 1, p. 275-383; v. 2, p. 385-782.
The true travels, 1630, v. 2, p. 805-916.

SOME VIRGINIA colonial records [1670?-1708]. Va. mag., 10 (1903), 371-82; continued to 11 (1903), 155-69.

STEWART, ROBERT A. Excerpts from the Charles City county records (1665-1666). Va. mag., 42 (1934), 341-44; continued to 43 (1935), 347-54.

STEWART, MRS. VICTOR W. Notes from Surry county records of the seventeenth century. W & M quar. (ser. 2), 19 (1939), 531-32.

STOCK, LEO F., ed. Proceedings and debates of the British parliaments respecting North America. Washington, 1924-1942. 5 v. (Carnegie inst. of Washington, publication no. 338) v. 1: 1542-1688. v. 2: 1689-1702.

THURLOE, JOHN. A collection of the state papers of John Thurloe . . . containing authentic memorials of the English affairs from the year 1638, to the restoration of King Charles II. London, 1742. 7 v.

TYLER, LYON G., ed. Narratives of early Virginia, 1606-1625. N. Y., 1907. 478 p.

Contents: Observations by Master George Percy, 1607. A true relation, by Capt. John Smith, 1608. Description of Virginia and

40

proceedings of the colonie by Captain John Smith, 1612. The relation of the Lord De-la-Ware, 1611. Letter of Don Diego de Molina, 1613. Letter of Father Pierre Biard, 1614. Letter of John Rolfe, 1614. Proceedings of the Virginia assembly, 1619. Letter of John Pory, 1619. The generall historie of Virginia by Captain John Smith, 1624, the fourth booke. The Virginia planters' answer to Captain Butler, 1623. The tragical relation of the Virginia assembly, 1624. The discourse of the old company, 1625.

TYLER's QUARTERLY historical and genealogical magazine. Richmond, 1919-1952. 33 v.

v. 1-10, indexed in E. G. Swem, Virginia historical index.

VIRGINIA. Calendar of Virginia state papers and other manuscripts . . . preserved in the capitol at Richmond. Richmond, 1875-93. 11 v.

v. 1, 1652-1781.
Indexed in E. G. Swem, Virginia historical index.

VIRGINIA (Colony). Council. Council papers, 1698-1701. Va. mag., 22 (1914), 29-43; continued to 23 (1915), 385-94.

_____Executive journals of the Council of colonial Virginia. Vol. 1 (June 11, 1680–June 22, 1699). Richmond, 1925. 587 p.

_____Legislative journals of the Council of colonial Virginia [1680-1775]. Richmond, 1918-19. 3 v.

_____Minutes of the council and general court of colonial Virginia, 1622-32, 1670-1676. Richmond, 1924. 593 p.

VIRGINIA (Colony) House of Burgesses. Journals, 1619–1658/59. Richmond, 1915. 283 p.

_____Journals, 1659/60–1693. Richmond, 1914. 529 p.
_____Journals, 1695/96–1700/02. Richmond, 1913. 414 p.

VIRGINIA COMPANY OF London. Abstract of the proceedings of the company, 1619-1624; prepared by Conway Robinson, ed. by R. A. Brock. Richmond, 1888-89. 2 v. (Virginia hist. soc., Collections, new ser., v. 7-8).

41

VIRGINIA HISTORICAL REGISTER, and literary companion; ed. by William Maxwell. Richmond, 1848-53. 6 v.

Indexed in E. G. Swem, Virginia historical index.

VIRGINIA IN 1623 [to 1681/82]. [Abstracts from the English Public record office and the McDonald and DeJarnette papers, Virginia state library, by W. N. Sainsbury.] Va. mag., 6 (1899), 236-44; continued to 29 (1921), 52-7.

VIRGINIA MAGAZINE OF history and biography. v. 1-to date. Richmond, 1893-to date.

v. 1-38, indexed in E. G. Swem, Virginia historical index.

VIRGINIA PAPERS, 1616-1619. [Collected by John Smith of Nibley, one of the early colonizers of Virginia.] N. Y. public library, Bulletin, 1 (1897), 68-72; continued to 3 (1899), 276-95.

WILLIAM AND MARY college quarterly historical magazine; ed. by Lyon G. Tyler [Ser. 1] Williamsburg, Va., 1892-1919. 27 v.

Second series, ed. by E. G. Swem, Williamsburg, Va., 1921-43. 23 v. Third series, ed. by R. L. Morton, and others, Williamsburg, Va., 1944-to date.
Ser. 1-2, v. 10, indexed in E. G. Swem, Virginia historical index.

WRIGHT, IRENE A., ed. Spanish policy toward Virginia, 1606-1612. Am. hist. rev., 25 (1920), 448-79.

WYATT, SIR FRANCIS. Documents of Sir Francis Wyatt, governor, 1621-1626. W & M quar. (ser. 2), 7 (1927), 42-7; continued to 8 (1928), 157-67.

BEFORE 1607

CANNER, THOMAS. A relation of the voyage made to Virginia, in the *Elizabeth* of London, a barke of fiftie tunnes by Captaine Bartholomew Gilbert, in the yeere 1603. In: Purchas his pilgrimes, v. 4, p. 1656-1658.

HARIOT, THOMAS. A brief and true report of the new found land of Virginia [1588; De Bry ed., 1590, with engravings of John White's drawings]. N. Y., 1871. 33 p., 47 l.

Reprinted: London, 1893. 111 p.; London, 1900. 84 p.; N. Y., 1903. 24 l.; [Monroe, N. C., n.d.] 48 p.; Ann Arbor, Mich., 1931. 48 p.

PRING, MARTIN. Scheepts-togt van Martin Pringe, gedaan in't jaar 1603. Van Bristol no't Noorder-gedeelte van Virginia. Leyden, 1706. 16 p.

PERCY, GEORGE. Observations gathered out of a discourse of the plantation of the southerne colonie in Virginia by the English, 1606. In: Purchas his pilgrimes, v. 4, p. 1685-1690.

Reprinted: John Smith, Travels and works, ed. by Arber, v. 1, p. lvii-lxxiii; Brown, Genesis of the U. S., v. 1, p. 152-68; Tyler, Narratives of early Virginia, p. 5-23.

STONEMAN, JOHN. The voyage of M. Henry Challons, intended for the North plantation of Virginia, 1606, taken by the way, and ill used by the Spaniards. In: Purchas his pilgrimes, v. 4, p. 1685-1690.

VIRGINIA. CHARTER. Part of the first patent granted by his maiestie for the plantation of Virginia, Aprill the tenth, 1606. In: Purchas his pilgrimes, v. 4, p. 1683-84.

VIRGINIA COMPANY OF LONDON. Instructions by way of advice, for the intended voyage to Virginia [1606]. In: John Smith, Travels and works, ed. by Arber, v. 1, p. xxxiii-xxxvii.

Reprinted: Neill, History of the London company of Virginia, p. 8-14.

1607-1609

[ARCHER, GABRIEL] Capt. Newport's discoveries, Virginia, May [1607]. A relatyon of the discovery of our river, from James forte into the maine. Am. antiq. soc., Trans., v. 4, (1860), p. 40-65.

Includes "The description of the now-discovered river and country of Virginia; with the liklyhood of ensuing ritches," p. 59-62.

"A brief description of the people," p. 63-65.
The "relatyon" itself is reprinted in John Smith, Travels and works, ed. by Arber, v. 1, p. xl-lv.

TINDALL, ROBERT. Robert Tindall, gunner to Prince Henry. Letter to the prince, 22 June 1607. In: John Smith, Travels and works, ed. by Arber, v. 1, p. xxxviii-xxxix.
Reprinted: Brown, Genesis of the U. S., v. 1, p. 108-9.

VIRGINIA. COUNCIL, 1607. Coppie of a letter from Virginia, dated 22d of June, 1607. In: Brown, Genesis of the U. S., v. 1, p. 106-8.

FORD, WORTHINGTON C. Tyndall's map of Virginia [1608]. Mass. hist. soc., Proc., 58 (1925), 244-47.
Includes facsimile reproduction.

SMITH, JOHN. The copy of a letter sent to the treasurer and councell of Virginia, [1608?]. In: Brown, Genesis of the U. S., v. 1, p. 199-204.

_____A true relation of such occurrences and accidents of noate as hath hapned in Virginia since the first planting of that collony, which is now resident in the south part thereof, till the last returne from thence. London, 1608. 36 p.
Reprinted: Boston, 1866. 88 p.; Smith, Travels and Works, ed. by Arber, v. 1, p. 1-40; Tyler, Narratives of early Virginia, p. 25-71.

WINGFIELD, EDWARD M. A discourse of Virginia [1608]; ed. with notes by Charles Deane. Boston, 1859. 44 p.
Reprinted: Am. antiq. soc., Transactions, 4 (1860), 67-103; John Smith, Travels and works, ed. by Arber, v. 1, p. lxxiv-xci.

[ARCHER, GABRIEL] A letter of M. Gabriel Archar, touching the voyage of the fleet of ships, which arrived at Virginia, without Sir Tho. Gates, and Sir George Summers, 1609. In: Purchas his pilgrimes, v. 4, p. 1733-34.
Reprinted: John Smith, Travels and works, ed. by Arber, v. 1, p. xciv-xcvii; Brown, Genesis of the U. S., v. 1, p. 328-32.

44

CRASHAW, WILLIAM. A sermon preached in London before the right honorable the Lord La Warre, Lord governour and Captaine generall of Virginea, and others of his Majesties counsell for that kingdome, and the rest of the adventurers in that plantation . . . Febr. 21, 1609. London, 1610. 91 p.

[GRAY, ROBERT] A good speed to Virginia. London, 1609. 29 p. Reprinted: N. Y., 1937. 43 p.

[JOHNSON, ROBERT] Nova Britannia. Offering most excellent fruites by planting in Virginia. London, 1609. 31 p.
Reprinted: Force tracts, v. 1, no. 6. 28 p.; N. Y., 1867. 40 p.

PRICE, DANIEL. Sauls prohibition staide; or, The apprehension and examination of Saule. And to the inditement of all that persecute Christ with a reproofe of those that traduce the honourable plantation of Virginia. London, 1609. 40 p.

RATCLIFFE, JOHN. Captain John Ratcliffe alias Sickelmore. Letter to the Earl of Salisbury, 4 October 1609. In: John Smith, Travels and works, ed. by Arber, v. 1, p. xcviii-xcix.

SYMONDS, WILLIAM. Virginia. A sermon preached at White-Chapel, in the presence of . . . the adventurers and planters for Virginia, 25. April. 1609. London, 1609. 54 p.

SPELMAN, HENRY. Relation of Virginia, 1609. London, 1872. 58 p.
Reprinted: John Smith, Travels and works, ed. by Arber, v. 1, p. ci-cxiv.

VIRGINIA COMPANY OF LONDON. [Advertising the enterprise un der the new charter. London? 1609] Broadside. In: Brown, First republic, p. 100-104.

____Instructions, orders and constitucions to Sir Thomas West, Knight, Lord La Warr. [1609?] In: Kingsbury, Records of the Virginia company, v. 3, p. 24-29.

____Instruccions, orders and constiticions to Sir Thomas Gates, Knight, Governor of Virginia. 1609. In: Kingsbury, Records of the Virginia company of London, v. 3, p. 12-24.

____A letter from the councill and company of the honourable plantation in Virginia to the Lord Mayor, alderman and companies of London [1609?]. In: Brown, Genesis of the U. S., v. 1, p. 252-54.

1610-1619

ARGALL, SIR SAMUEL. The voiage from James Towne to seeke the ile of Bermuda, and missing the same, his putting over toward Sagadahoc and Cape Cod, and so back againe to James Towne, begun the nineteenth of June, 1610. In: Purchas his pilgrimes, v. 4, p. 1758-62.

DE LA WARR, THOMAS WEST, 3rd lord. Lorde De la Warr to the right honorable . . . the Earl of Salisbury, 1610. In: Brown, Genesis of the U. S., v. 1, p. 413-15.

[JOURDAIN, SILVESTER] A discovery of the Barmudas, otherwise called the Ile of Divels; by Sir Thomas Gates, Sir George Sommers, and Captayne Newport, with divers others. London, 1610. In: Force tracts, v. 3, no. 3, p. 9-15

Reprinted N. Y., 1940. 24 p.

THE PROCEEDINGS OF the English colony in Virginia, from the beginning of the plantation 1606, till anno 1610, somewhat abridged. In: Purchas his pilgrimes, v. 4, p. 1705-33.

RICH [RICHARD] Newes from Virginia (1610). London, 1874. 19 p.

Reprinted: Neill, Early settlement of Virginia and Virginiola, p. 29-35; [Boston, 1922] 14 p. (Americana series, photostat, no. 65); [N. Y., 1937] 29 p.

STRACHEY, WILLIAM. A true reportory of the wracke, and redemption of Sir Thomas Gates, Knight; upon, and from the ilands of the Bermudas: his coming to Virginia, and the estate of that colonie then, and after, under the government of the Lord La Warr, July 15, 1610. In: Purchas his pilgrimes, v. 4, p. 1734-58.

VIRGINIA COMPANY OF LONDON. By the counsell of Virginea [Notice that the ship *Hercules* is now preparing to make a supply to the colony of Virginia] [London? 1610] Broadside. In: Brown, Genesis of the U. S., v. 1, p. 439.

_____A publication by the counsell of Virginea, touching the plantation there. London, 1610. Broadside. In: Brown, Genesis of the U. S., v. 1, p. 354-356.

_____A true and sincere declaration of the purpose and ends of the plantation begun in Virginia. London, 1610. 26 p.
Reprinted: Brown, Genesis of the U. S., v. 1, p. 338-53.

_____A true declaration of the estate of the colonie in Virginia, with a confutation of such scandalous reports as have tended to the disgrace of so worthy an enterprise. London, 1610. 68 p.
Reprinted: Force tracts, v. 3, no. 1. 27 p.

VIRGINIA. COUNCIL, 1610. Letter of the Governor and council of Virginia to the Virginia company of London. In: Brown, Genesis of the U. S., v. 1, p. 402-13.

DALE, SIR THOMAS. Letter to Lord Salisbury, 1611. In: Brown, Genesis of the U. S., v. 1, p. 501-8.

_____Sir Thomas Dale to the president and counsell of the companie of adventurers and planters in Virginia [1611]. In: Brown, Genesis of the U. S., v. 1, p. 489-94.

DE LA WARR, THOMAS WEST, 3rd lord. The relation of the right honourable the Lord De la Warre. London, 1611. 15 p.
Reprinted: N. Y. [1868?] 17 p.; [London, 1858] 17p.; Tyler,

47

Narratives of early Virginia, 209-214; Brown, Genesis of the U. S., v. 1, p. 477-83.

DEPOSITIONS OF John Clarke and others, at Havana, 1611. Am. hist. rev., 25 (1920), 467-73.

VIRGINIA COMPANY OF LONDON. By the counsell of Virginea. [That a fleet of good ships would soon be ready to sail for Virginia.] London, 1611. Broadside. In: Brown, Genesis of the U. S., v. 1, p. 445.

WHITAKER, ALEXANDER. Whitaker to Crashaw . . . 1611. In: Brown, Genesis of the U. S., v. 1, p. 497-500.

EXPERIENCES ON JOURNEY to America. Accurate transcript from the Booke of proceedings and accidents of the first permanent English settlement in America [1612] Connecticut mag., 11 (1907), 315-19.
Reprinted: Journal of Am. hist., 1 (1907), 206-8.

[JOHNSON, ROBERT] The new life of Virginea: declaring the former successe and present estate of that plantation, being the second part of Nova Britannia. London, 1612. 52 p.
Reprinted: Force tracts, v. 1, no. 7. 24 p.; Mass. hist. soc., Collections (ser. 2), 8 (1826), 199-223.

McCARY, BEN C. Captain John Smith's map of Virginia [1612]. Williamsburg, 1957. (Jamestown 350th anniversary historical booklet, No. 3.)

PERCY, GEORGE. "A trewe relacyon." Virginia from 1609-1612. Tyler's quarterly, 3 (1922), 259-82.

THE PROCEEDINGS AND ACCIDENTS of the English colony in Virginia, extracted from the authors following, by William Simons, doctour of divinitie [1612] In: John Smith, Travels and works, ed. by Arber, v. 2, p. 383-488.

THE PROCEEDINGS OF the English colonie in Virginia since their first beginning from England in the yeere of our Lord 1606, till this present 1612, with all their accidents that befell them in their journies and discoveries. By W. S. Oxford, 1612. In: John Smith, Travels and works, ed. by Arber, v. 1, p. 85-174.

Reprinted: Tyler, Narratives of early Virginia, p. 119-204.

SMITH, JOHN. The description of Virginia by Captaine John Smith, inlarged out of his written notes. In: Purchas his pilgrimes, v. 4, p. 1691-1704.

_____A map of Virginia. With a description of the countrey, the commodities, people, government and religion. Oxford, 1612, 39, 110 p.

Reprinted: Smith, Travels and works, ed. by Arber, v. 1, p. 41-174; Tyler, Narratives of early Virginia, p. 76-204.
Contents: [Vocabulary of Indian words.] The description of Virginia. The proceedings of the English colonie in Virginia . . . till this present 1612.

[STRACHEY, WILLIAM, ed.] For the colony in Virginea Britannia. Lawes divine, morall and martiall. London, 1612. 41, 7 p.

Reprinted: Force tracts, v. 3, no. 2. 68 p.; Photostat Americana, ser. 2, no. 16, Boston, 1936.

_____The historie of travell into Virginia Britania (1612); ed. by Louis B. Wright and Virginia Freund. London, 1953. xxxii, 221 p.

Also ed. by R. H. Major, London, 1849. 203 p.

ARGALL, SIR SAMUEL. A letter touching his voyage to Virginia, and actions there, written to Nicholas Hawes, June, 1613. In: Purchas his pilgrimes, v. 4, p. 1764-65.

Reprinted: Brown, Genesis of the U. S., v. 2, p. 640-44.

DALE, SIR THOMAS. Sir Thomas Dale's letter to Sir Thomas Smith, 1613. Extract in: Brown, Genesis of the U. S., v. 2, p. 639-40.

[JOURDAIN, SILVESTER] A plaine description of the Barmudas, now called Sommer Ilands. With the manner of their discoverie Anno 1609. London, 1613. 43 p.

Reprinted: Force tracts, v. 3, no. 3. 24 p.

VIRGINIA COMPANY OF LONDON. A broadside [concerning the lottery] 1613. In: Brown, Genesis of the U. S., v. 2, p. 608-9.

____By his Majesties councell for Virginia [On the lottery to be held May 10, 1613] London, 1613. Broadside. In: Brown, Genesis of the U. S., v. 2, p. 608-9; John Carter Brown Library, Three proclamations.

WHITAKER, ALEXANDER. Good newes from Virginia. London, 1613. 14, 44 p.

Reprinted: [N. Y., 1936] 14, 44 p.

____Part of a tractate written at Henrico in Virginia, 1613. In: Purchas his pilgrimes, v. 4, p. 1771-73.

DALE, SIR THOMAS. A letter of Sir Thomas Dale, and another of Master Whitakers, from James Towne in Virginia, June 18, 1614. And a piece of a tractate, written by the said Master Whitakers from Virginia the yeere before. In: Purchas his pilgrimes, v. 4, p. 1768-1773.

HAMOR, RALPH. Notes of Virginia affaires in the government of Sir Thomas Dale and of Sir Thomas Gates till anno 1614. In: Purchas his pilgrimes, v. 4, p. 1766-68.

____A true discourse of the present estate of Virginia, and the successe of the affaires there till the 18 of June, 1614. Together with a relation of the severall English townes and forts, the assured hopes of that countrie and the peace concluded with the Indians. The Christening of Powhatans daughter and her marriage with an English-man. London, 1615. 69 p.

Reprinted: Albany, N. Y., 1860. 69 p.

ROLFE, JOHN. The coppie of the Gentle-mans letters to Sir Thomas Dale, that after married Powhatans daughter, containing the reasons moving him thereunto [1614] In: Tyler, Narratives of early Virginia, p. 239-44.

VIRGINIA COMPANY OF LONDON. The reply of the Virginia council, 1614, in defense of Argall. In: Brown, Genesis of the U. S., v. 2, p. 730-33.

____A declaration for the certain time of drawing the great standing lottery. London, 1615. Broadside. In: Brown, Genesis of the U. S., v. 2, p. 684-685, 761-765; also in John Carter Brown library, Three proclamations.

ROLFE, JOHN. A true relation of the state of Virginia lefte by Sir Thomas Dale, knight, in May last, 1616. From original manuscript in the library of Henry C. Taylor, Esq. Edited by J. C. Wylie, F. L. Berkeley, Jr., and John M. Jennings. New Haven, Conn., 1951. 29 p.
   Printed earlier in Southern literary messenger, 5 (1839), 401-6; reprinted Va., historical register, 1 (1848), 101-13.

SMITH, JOHN. Captain John Smith to Queen Anne [1616?] In: Brown, Genesis of the U. S., v. 2, p. 784-88.

VIRGINIA COMPANY OF LONDON. A briefe declaration of the present state of things in Virginia [1616] In: Brown, Genesis of the U. S., v. 2, p. 774-79.

ROLFE, JOHN. Letter of John Rolfe [to Edwin Sandys, 8 June], 1617. Va. mag., 10 (1902), 134-138.

VIRGINIA COMPANY OF LONDON. By his Majesties councell for Virginia [relating the good condition of the colony at the return of Sir Thomas Dale] [London? 1617] Broadside. In: Brown, Genesis of the U. S., v. 2, p. 797-798.

ADVENTURERS TO VIRGINIA [1618?]. In: Kingsbury, Records of the Virginia company, v. 3, p. 79-90.

VIRGINIA COMPANY OF LONDON. Instructions to George Yeardley, 1618. In: Kingsbury, Records of the Virginia company, v. 3, p. 98-109.

OF THE LOTTERY: Sir Thomas Dales returne: the Spaniards in Virginia. Of Pocahontas and Tomocomo: Captaine Yerdley and Captaine Argoll (both since knights) their government; the Lord La-Warrs death, and other occurrents till anno 1619. In: Purchas his pilgrimes, v. 4, p. 1773-75.

PORY, JOHN. Letter of John Pory, 1619 secretary of Virginia, to Sir Dudley Carleton. In: Tyler, Narratives of early Virginia, p. 282-87.

VIRGINIA. ASSEMBLY, 1619. A reporte of the manner of proceedings in the General assembly convened at James citty in Virginia, July 30, 1619. N. Y., hist. soc., Collections (ser. 2), 3 (1857), 329-58.

> Reprinted: Colonial Records of Virginia, p. 9-32; Tyler, Narratives of early Virginia, p. 249-78; Kingsbury, Records of the Virginia company, v. 3, p. 153-77.

VIRGINIA COMPANY OF LONDON. A note of the shipping, men, and provisions sent to Virginia. London, 1619. 3 p.

> Reprinted: Brown, First republic, p. 366; Va. mag., 6 (1898), 231-32; Kingsbury, Records of the Virginia company, v. 3, p. 115-17.

YATE, FERDINANDO. Yate's account of a voyage to Virginia in 1619. N. Y. public library, Bulletin, 1 (1897), 68-72.

> Reprinted: Kingsbury, Records of the Virginia company, v. 3, p. 109-14.

1620-1629

[BUTLER, NATHANIEL] Historye of the Bermudaes or Summer islands [162-?] Ed. from a Ms. in the Sloane collection, British museum, by J. H. Lefroy. London, 1882. 327 p. (Hakluyt soc., Works, no. 65)

[BONOEIL, JOHN] Observations to be followed, for the making of fit roomes, to keepe silke-wormes in: as also, for the best manner of planting of mulberry trees, to feed them. London, 1620. 28 p.

"A valuation of the commodities growing and to be had in Virginia, rated as they are worth," p. 25-8.

CHESTER, ANTHONY. Scheeps-togt van Anthony Chester, na Virginia. Gedaan in het jaar 1620. Leyden, 1907. 15 p.

Translation by C. E. Bishop in W & M quar. (ser. 1), 9 (1901), 203-14.

JAMES I. King of Great Britain. By the King [a proclamation discontinuing the lotteries for the benefit of the colony of Virginia] London, 1620. Broadside.

Reprinted: Brown univ., John Carter Brown library, Three proclamations; Kingsbury, Records of the Virginia company, v. 3, p. 434-35.

PURCHAS, SAMUEL. The estate of the colony, A.D., 1620. In: Purchas his pilgrimes, v. 4, p. 1775-1779.

VIRGINIA COMPANY OF LONDON. A declaration of the state of the colonie and affaires in Virginia. London, 1620. 92 p.

Reprinted: Force tracts, v. 3, no. 5. 44, 26 p. Kingsbury, Records of the Virginia company, v. 3, p. 307-65.

____A note of the shipping, men and provisions sent and provided for Virginia [London? 1620]. In: Kingsbury, Records of the Virginia company, v. 3, p. 239-40.

____Orders and constitutions, partly collected out of his Maiesties letters patents, and partly ordained upon mature deliberation by the treasuror, counceil and companie of Virginia. Anno 1619 and 1620. In: Force tracts, v. 3, no. 6. 26 p.

____Treasuror, councell, and company for Virginia. [On the condition of the colony.] [London, 1620] Broadside.

Reprinted: Kingsbury, Records of the Virginia company, v. 3, p. 275-80.

GREEVOUS GRONES FOR the poore. Done by a well-willer, who wisheth, that the poore of England might be so provided for, as none should neede to go a begging within this realme. London, 1621. 24 p.

NEWS FROM VIRGINIA in letters sent thence 1621, partly published by the company, partly transcribed from the originals with letters of his maiestie, and of the company, touching silke-workes. In: Purchas his pilgrimes, v. 4, p. 1785-88.

ROLFE, JOHN. The will of John Rolfe [Jamestown, 10 March, 1621. Edited] by Jane Carson. Va. Mag., 58 (1950), 58-65.

A TRUE RELATION OF A sea fight between two great and well appointed Spanish ships, or men of warre; and an English ship . . . going for Virginia [1621] In: Purchas his pilgrimes, v. 4, p. 1780-82.
    Reprinted: Brown, First republic, p. 415-16.

THE ANSWERS OF divers planters . . . unto a paper intituled The unmasked face of our colony in Virginia. 1622. In: Kingsbury, Records of the Virginia company, v. 2, p. 381-86.

THE BARBAROUS MASSACRE committed by the savages on the English planters, March the two and twentieth, 1622, after the English accompt. In: Purchas his pilgrimes, v. 4, p. 1788-90.

[BONOEIL, JOHN] His Maiesties gracious letter to the Earle of South-Hampton, treasurer, and to the councell and company of Virginia heere; commanding the present setting up of silke-works, and planting of vines in Virginia. London, 1622. 88 p.

BRINSLEY, JOHN. A consolation for our grammar schooles: or, A faithfull and most comfortable incouragement, for laying of a sure foundation of all good learning in our schooles, and for prosperous building thereupon. More especially for all those of the inferiour sort, and all ruder countries and places; namely, for Ireland, Wales, Virginia, with the Sommer Ilands. London [1622] 84 p.

Reprinted: N. Y., 1943. 84 p.

BUTLER, NATHANIEL. The unmasked face of our colony in Virginia as it was in the winter of the yeare 1622. In: Kingsbury, Records of the Virginia company, v. 2, p. 374-76.

COPLAND, PATRICK. A declaration how the monies (viz. seventy pound eight shillings sixe pence) were disposed, which was gathered (by M. Patrick Copland, preacher in the Royall James) at the Cape of good hope, (towards the building of a free schoole in Virginia) of the gentle men and marriners in the said ship . . . London, 1622, [8] p.

Reprinted: Kingsbury, Records of the Virginia company, v. 3, p. 537-40.

_____Virginia's God be thanked; or, A sermon of thanksgiving for the happie successe of the affayres in Virginia this last yeare. London, 1622. 36 p.

DONNE, JOHN. A sermon upon the VIII. verse of the I chapter of the Acts of the Apostles. Preach'd to the honourable company of the Virginian plantation, 13 Novemb. 1622. London, 1622. 49 p.

VIRGINIA COMPANY OF LONDON. The inconveniences that have happened to some persons which have transported themselves from England to Virginia. London, 1622. Broadside. In: Brown, First republic, 486-87.

WATERHOUSE, EDWARD. A declaration of the state of the colony and affaires in Virginia. London, 1622. 54 p.

Reprinted: Kingsbury, Records of the Virginia company, v. 3, p. 541-79.

AN ANSWERE TO a declaracion of the present state of Virginia,

May, 1623. In: Kingsbury, Records of the Virginia company, v. 4, p. 130-151.

A FORME OF POLISIE to plant and governe many families in Virginia [1623]. Am. hist. rev., 19 (1914), 560-78.
Reprinted: Kingsbury, Records of the Virginia company, v. 4, p. 408-35.

NEWTON, ARTHUR P., ed. A new plan to govern Virginia, 1623. Am. hist. rev., 19 (1914), 559-78.

A NOTE OF PROVISIONS necessarie for every planter or personall adventurer to Virginia: and accidents since the massacre. In: Purchas his pilgrimes, v. 4, p. 1791-93.

PURCHAS, SAMUEL. Of Virginia. In: Purchas his pilgrimes, v. 5, p. 828-45.

NOTES TAKEN FROM letters which came from Virginia [1623]. In: Kingsbury, Records of the Virginia company, v. 4, p. 228-239.

SMITH, JOHN (1580-1631). The generall history of Virginia, the Somer Iles, and New England, with the names of the adventurers and their adventures. . . . [A prospectus]. [n.p., 1623?] 4 p.

THE VIRGINIA PLANTERS' answer to Captain Butler, 1623. In: Neill, Virginia company of London, 395-404.
Reprinted: Kingsbury, Records of the Virginia company of London, v. 2, p. 381-85; Tyler, Narratives of early Virginia, p. 412-18.

WYATT, SIR FRANCIS. Letter of Sir Francis Wyatt [1623?]. W & M quar. (ser. 2), 6 (1926), 114-21.

GOOD NEWS FROM Virginia, sent from James his town by a gentleman in that country. London [1624?]. W & M quar. (ser. 3), 5 (1948), 353-58.

56

HARVEY, JOHN. A brief declaration of the state of Virginia, 1624. Mass. hist. soc., Collections (ser. 4), 9 (1871), 60-81.

JAMES I. King of Great Britain. A proclamation concerning tobacco [restraining importation of tobacco except from Virginia and the Somers islands] London, 1624. 4 p.

Reprinted: Hazard, Historical collections, v. 1, p. 193-98.

QUO WARRANTO AND proceedings, by which the Virginia company was dissolved [1623-24]. In: Kingsbury, Records of the Virginia company, v. 4, p. 295-358; translation from Latin, 358-98.

ARGALL, SIR SAMUEL. Briefe intelligence from Virginia letters, a supplement of French-Virginian occurants, and their supplantation by Sir Samuel Argal, in right of the English plantation [in the year 1624]. In: Purchas his pilgrimes, v. 4, p. 1805-9.

VIRGINIA'S VERGER: or, A discourse shewing the benefits which may grow to this kingdome from American English plantations, and specially those of Virginia and Summer Islands. In: Purchas his pilgrimes, v. 4, p. 1809-26.

SMITH, JOHN. The generall historie of Virginia, New-England, and the Summer Isles. London, 1624. 248 p.

Reissued 1625, 1626, 1627, 1631, 1632. Reprinted, Richmond, 1819. 2 v.; London, 1884, 2 v.; Glasgow, 1907, 2 v.; Edinburgh, 1910, 2 v.

VIRGINIA. Assembly, 1624. The tragical relation of the Virginia assembly, 1624. In: Tyler, Narratives of early Virginia, p. 422-26.

CHARLES I, King of Great Britain. By the King: a proclamation for setling the plantation of Virginia [1625]. With an intro. by Thomas C. Johnson. Charlottesville, Va., 1946. 39 p.

CONSIDERATIONS TOUCHING the new contract for tobacco, [London] 1625. 11 p.

Reproduced: Americana series, no. 94 (photostat).

JAMES I. King of Great Britain. A proclamation for the utter prohibiting the importation and use of all tobacco which is not the proper growth of the collonyes of Virginia and the Sommer islands, or one of them [1625]. In: Hazard, Historical collections, v. 1, p. 224-30.

VIRGINIA COMPANY OF LONDON. The discourse of the old company, 1625. Va. mag., 1 (1894), 155-67, 287-309.

Reprinted: Tyler, Narratives of early Virginia, p. 431-60; Kingsbury, Records of the Virginia company, v. 4, p. 519-551.

HULSIUS, LEVINUS. Zwantzigste schifffahrt, oder grundliche . . beschreibung desz Newen Engellands . . . der landtschaffi Virginia, und der insel Barmuda. Franckfurt, 1629.

Von der landtschafft Virginia, p. 39-116.

SMITH, JOHN. The true travels, adventures and observations of Captaine John Smith, in Europe, Asia, Africke, and America: beginning about the yeere 1593, and continued to this present 1629. London, 1630. 60 p.

Reprinted: Richmond, 1819. 2 v.; In his: Travels and works, ed. by Arber, v. 2, 805-916; N. Y., 1930. 80 p.

1630-1639

CHARLES I, King of Great Britain. By the King; a proclamation concerning tobacco. London [1631]. Broadside.

Reprinted: Richmond, 1952.

FLEET, HENRY. A brief journal of a voyage made in the bark "Warwick" to Virginia [1631]. In: Neill, English colonization of America, p. 221-37.

Smith, John. Advertisements for the unexperienced planters of New-England, or any where; or, The path-way to experience to erect a plantation. London, 1631. 40 p.

Reprinted: Mass. hist. soc., Collections (ser. 3), 3 (1833), 1-53; John Smith, Travels and works, ed. by Arber, v. 2, p. 917-66.

Smith, John. The last will and testament of Captain John Smith [1631]; with some additional memoranda relating to him [by Charles Deane]. Cambridge, Mass., 1867. 7 p.

Reprinted: Mass. hist. soc., Proceedings (1867), p. 452-56.

[Sandys, George, trans.] Ovid's Metamorphosis Englished, mythologiz'd, and represented in figures. Oxford, 1632. 525 p.

Yong, Thomas. Voyage to Virginia and Delaware Bay and river in 1634. Mass. hist. soc., Collections (ser. 4), 9 (1871), 81-131.

[Goodborne, John] A Virginian minister's library, 1635; ed. by R. G. Marsden. Am. hist. rev., 11 (1906), 328-32.

Somerby, H. G. Passengers for Virginia, 1635. New England hist. and gen. register, 2 (1848), 111-13; continued to 5 (1851), 343-44, and 15 (1861), 142-46.

Hiden, Martha W. Accompts of the *Tristram and Jane* [a ship arriving at Virginia, 1637]. Va. mag., 62 (1954), 424-47.

1640-1649

Extract from a manuscript collection of annals relative to Virginia [in 1642]. Force tracts, v. 2, no. 6. 9 p.

A servant in England to his master in Virginia [1642]. W & M quar. (ser. 1), 11 (1903), 243-44.

Vries, David Pietersz de. Voyages from Holland to America,

A.D. 1632 to 1644, trans. from the Dutch by Henry C. Murphy. N. Y., 1853. 199 p.

Reprinted: N. Y. hist. soc., Collections (ser. 2), 3 (1857), 1-136.

CASTELL, WILLIAM. A short discoverie of the coasts and continent of America, from the equinoctiall northward, and of the adjacent isles. London, 1644. 112 p.

LEWIS, CLIFFORD, ed. Some recently discovered extracts from the lost minutes of the Virginia council and general court, 1642-1645. W & M quar. (ser. 2), 20 (1939), 62-78.

GREAT BRITAIN. Two ordinances of the Lords and Commons assembled in Parliament [1643, 1645]. Whereby Robert Earle of Warwick is made governor in chief, and L. high admirall of all those islands and other plantations . . . within the bounds, and upon the coasts of America. London, 1645. [Boston, 1926] 6 p. (Americana series photostat, no. 159)

A DESCRIPTION OF THE province of New Albion. And a direction for adventurers with small stock to get two for one, and good land freely: and for gentlemen, and all servants, labourers and artificers to live plentifully . . . 1648. Force tracts, v. 2, no. 7. 35 p.

BULLOCK, WILLIAM. Virginia impartially examined, and left to publick view, to be considered by all judicious and honest men. London, 1649. 66 p.

[NORWOOD, HENRY] A voyage to Virginia [1649]. In: Force tracts, v. 3, no. 10. 50 p.

A PERFECT DESCRIPTION of Virginia: being, a full and true relation of the present state of the plantation . . . Also, a narration of the countrey, within a few dayes journey of Virginia, west and by south. [London, 1649] Mass. hist. soc., Collections (ser. 2), 9 (1832), 105-22.

Reprinted: Force tracts, v. 2, no. 8. 18 p.

1650-1659

Scisco, Louis D. Exploration of 1650 in southern Virginia. Tyler's quar., 7 (1926), 164-69.

Williams, Edward. Virgo triumphans: or, Virginia richly and truly valued; more especially the south part thereof: viz. the fertile Carolana, and no lesse excellent isle of Roanoak, of latitude from 31 to 37 degr. relating the meanes of raising infinite profits to the adventurers and planters. London, 1650. 7, 47 p.

_____Virginia: more especially the south part thereof, richly and truly valued. 2nd ed. London, 1650. 47 p.

First edition entitled: Virgo triumphans; or, Virginia richly and truly valued.

Reprinted: Force tracts, v. 3, no. 11. 62 p.

_____Virginia's discovery of silke-wormes with their benefit. And the implanting of mulberry trees. Also the dressing and keeping of vines, for the rich trade of making wines there. Together with the making of the saw-mill, very useful in Virginia, for cutting of timber and clapbord, to build withall. London, 1650. 75 p.

Part 2 of his Virginia: more especially the south part thereof, richly and truly valued.

An act prohibiting trade with the Barbada's, Virginia, Bermudas and Antego. London, 1650. In: A collection of several acts of Parliament, 1648-1651, ed. by H. Scobell, London, 1651.

Reprinted: Hazard, Historical collections, v. 1, p. 636-38.

An act of indempnitie made att the surrender of the countrey

[March 12, 1651]. In: Jefferson, Notes on Virginia; ed. by Peden, p. 116-17.

Reprinted: Hazard, Historical collections, v. 1, p. 563-64.

AN ACT FOR increase of shipping, and encouragement of the navigation of this nation. In: A collection of several acts of Parliament, 1648-1651, ed. by H. Scobell, London, 1651.

Reprinted: William MacDonald, ed., Select charters and other documents illustrative of American history, 1606-1775, N. Y., 1910, p. 106-110.

ARTICLES AGREED ON & concluded at James Cittie in Virginia for the surrendering and settling of that plantation under the obedience & goverment of the common wealth of England by the Commissioners of the Councill of state . . . & by the Grand assembly . . . of that countrey [1651]. In: Jefferson, Notes on Virginia, ed. by Peden, p. 114-16.

Reprinted: Hazard, Historical collections, v. 1, p. 560-61.

BESCHRIJVINGHE VAN VIRGINIA, Nieuw Nederlandt, Nieuw Engelandt, en d'Eylanden Bermudes, Berbados en S. Christoffel. Amsterdam, 1651. 88 p.

[BLAND, EDWARD, and others] The discovery of New Brittaine. Began August 27, Anno. Dom. 1650 . . . From Fort Henry, at the head of Appamattuck river in Virginia, to the fals of Blandina, first river in New Brittaine. London, 1651. 16 p.

Reprinted: N. Y., 1873. 16 p.; Alvord and Bidgood, The first explorations of the trans-Allegheny region, p. 114-30; Ann Arbor, Mich., 1954. 10, 16 p.

COPY OF A PETITION from the governor and company of the Summer islands, with annexed papers . . . with a short collection of . . . passages from the original to the dissolution of the Virginia company, and a large description of Virginia. London, 1651. 30, 20 p.

SOMERS ISLANDS COMPANY. Copy of a petition from the governor and company of the Sommer islands. With annexed papers

. . . And a large description of Virginia, with the several commodities thereof. London, 1651. 30 p.

[WODENOTH, ARTHUR] A short collection of the most remarkable passages from the originall to the dissolution of the Virginia company. London, 1651. 20 p.

BERKELEY, SIR WILLIAM. The speech of the Hon. William Berkeley . . . to the burgesses in the Grand assembly at James Towne on the 17 of March 1651/2. Va. mag., 1 (1893), 75-81.

[HARTLIB, SAMUEL] Glory be to God on high, peace on earth, good will amongst men. A rare and new discovery of a speedy way, and easie means, found out by a young lady in England, she having made full proofe thereof in May, Anno 1652, for the feeding of silk-worms in the woods, on the mulberry-tree-leaves in Virginia. [London] 1652. 12 p.

WITHINGTON, LOTHROP. Surrender of Virginia to the parliamentary commissioners, March, 1651/52. Va. mag., 11 (1903), 32-41.

THE LORD BALTEMORE'S case, concerning the province of Maryland. Adjoyning to Virginia in America. With full and clear answers to all material objections, touching his rights, jurisdiction, and proceedings there. London, 1653. 20 p.
    Reprinted: Hall, Narratives of early Maryland, 167-80.

[HARTLIB, SAMUEL] The reformed Virginian silk-worm, or, A rare and new discovery of a speedy way, and easie means, found out by a young lady in England, she having made full proof thereof in May, anno 1652. London, 1655. 40 p.
    Reprinted: Force tracts, v. 3, no. 13. 37 p.

VIRGINIA AND MARYLAND. Or, The Lord Baltamore's printed case, uncased and answered. Showing the illegality of his patent and usurpation of royal jurisdiction and dominion there. London, 1655. 52 p.

Reprinted: Force tracts, v. 2, no. 9. 47 p.; Hall, Narratives of early Maryland, 187-230.

HAMMOND, JOHN. Leah and Rachel or, The two fruitfull sisters Virginia, and Maryland; their present condition, impartially stated and related. London, 1656. 32 p.

Reprinted: Force tracts, v. 3, no. 14. 30 p.; Hall, Narratives of early Maryland, p. 281-308.

[GATFORD, LIONEL] Publick good without private interest. Or, A compendious remonstrance of the present sad state and condition of the English colonie in Virginea. London, 1657. [Paris, 1866] 8, 26 p.

GORGES, FERDINANDO. America painted to the life. The true history of the Spaniards proceedings in the conquests of the Indians . . . an absolute narrative of the north parts of America, and of the discoveries and plantations of our English in Virginia, New-England, and Berbadoes. London, 1658-59. 4 pts. in 1 v.

Pt. 2 "A briefe narration of the originall undertakings of the advancement of plantations into the parts of America," reprinted: J. P. Baxter, ed., Sir Ferdinando Gorges and his province of Maine, v. 2, p. 1-81.

1660-1669

BLAND, JOHN. To the Kings most excellent majesty; the humble remonstrance of John Blande of London, merchant, on the behalf of the inhabitants and planters in Virginia and Mariland. [London? 1661?] [Boston, 1940] 4 p. (Photostat Americana, ser. 2, no. 100)

[GRAVE, JOHN] A song of Sion. Written by a citizen thereof, whose outward habitation is in Virginia. [London, 1662] 12 p.

[GREENE, ROBERT] Virginia's cure: or, An advisive narrative concerning Virginia. Discovering the true ground of that churches unhappiness, and the only true remedy. London, 1662. 22 p.

Reprinted: Force tracts, v. 3, no. 15. 19 p.

VIRGINIA. General assembly. The lawes of Virginia now in force: collected out of the Assembly records, and digested into one volume. Revised and confirmed by the grand assembly held at James-City, by prorogation, the 23d of March, 1661. London, 1662. 82 p.

BERKELEY, SIR WILLIAM. A discourse and view of Virginia. London, 1663. [Norwalk, Conn., 1914] 8, 12 p.

SCARBURGH, EDMOND. Document presented by C. C. Harper, Esq., from the Committee on the library, enclosing Col. Edmond Scarburgh's account of proceedings in an expedition from Virginia to Annamessecks and Manokin, pursuant to an act of the Grand assembly of Virginia, in the year 1663. Annapolis, Md., 1833. 16 p.

MORAY, ALEXANDER. Letters written from Ware river in Mockjack bay, Virginia, Feb. 1, 1665. W & M quar. (ser. 2), 2 (1922), 157-61.

[LUDWELL, THOMAS] A description of the government of Virginia [1666]. Va. mag., 5 (1897), 54-59.

ATTACKS BY THE Dutch on the Virginia fleet in Hampton Roads in 1667. Va. mag., 4 (1897), 229-45.

STRANGE NEWS FROM Virginia, being a true relation of a great tempest in Virginia, by which many people lost their lives, great numbers of cattle destroyed, houses, and in many places whole plantations overturned, and whole woods torn up by the roots. London, 1667. 7 p.

Shrigley, Nathaniel. A true relation of Virginia and Maryland; with the commodities therein. London, 1669. In: Force tracts, v. 3, no. 7. 5 p.

Revel, James. "The poor unhappy transported felon's sorrowful account of his fourtteen years transportation, at Virginia, in America [1656?-1671?]" Reprinted, with introductory notes by John M. Jennings. Va. Mag., 56 (1948), 180-194.

1670-1679

[Fallows, Robert.] The expedition of Batts and Fallam. John Clayton's transcript of the journal of Robert Fallam. A journal from Virginia, beyond the Apailachian mountains, in Sept. 1671. Sent to the Royal society by Mr. Clayton, and read Aug. 1, 1688, before the said society. In: Alvord and Bidgood, the first explorations of the Trans-Allegheny region, p. 183-205.

Reprinted: Am. anthropologist (new ser.), 9 (1907), 46-53.

_____The journal & relation of a new discovery made behind the Apuleian mountains to the west of Virginia [1671]. In: Documents relative to the col. hist. of the state of N. Y., v. 3 (1853), p. 193-97.

Ogilby, John. America: being the latest, and most accurate description of the New World; containing the original of the inhabitants, and the remarkable voyages thither. London, 1671. 674 p.

Lederer, John. The discoveries of John Lederer, in three several marches from Virginia to the west of Carolina . . . from the original edition of 1672. Cincinnati, O., 1879. 33 p.

Reprinted: Charleston, S. C., 1891. 47 p.; Rochester, N. Y., 1902. 30 p.

AN ACCOUNT OF the advantage of Virginia for building ships. Communicated by an observing gentleman. Royal society of London, Philos. trans., Apr. 21, 1673, p. 6015-16.

PHILLIPS, PHILIP L. The rare map of Virginia and Maryland [1673] by Augustine Herrman. Washington, 1911. 23 p.

THE KID-NAPPER TRAPAN'D: or, The treacherous husband caught in his own trap. Being a pleasant and true relation of a man in this town that would have sold his wife to Virginia. London, 1675. 7 p.

BACON, NATHANIEL. Proclamations of Nathaniel Bacon [1676]. Va. mag., 1 (1893), 55-63.

BACON'S REBELLION [accounts by William Sherwood and Philip Ludwell]. Va. mag., 1 (1893), 167-86.

BERKELEY, SIR WILLIAM. A list of those that have been executed for the late rebellion in Virginia. In: Force tracts, v. 1, no. 10. 4 p.

COTTON, MRS. ANNE. An account of our late troubles in Virginia. Written in 1676. In: Force tracts, v. 1, no. 9. 12 p.

GLOVER, THOMAS. An account of Virginia . . . reprinted from the Philosophical transactions of the Royal society, June 20, 1676. Oxford, 1904. 31 p.

GRANTHAM, SIR THOMAS. An historical account of some memorable actions, particularly in Virginia [1676]. London, 1716. Richmond, 1882. 71 p.

THE HISTORY OF Bacon's and Ingram's rebellion in Virginia, in 1675 and 1676. Mass. hist. soc., Proceedings (1866), 299-342.

> Reprinted: Cambridge, Mass., 1867. 50 p.; Andrews, Narratives of the insurrections, p. 47-98.

[MATHEW, THOMAS] The beginning, progress, and conclusion of Bacon's rebellion in Virginia in the years 1675 and 1676. In: Force tracts, v. 1, no. 8. 26 p.

Reprinted: Andrews, Narratives of the insurrections, p. 15-41.

MORE NEWS FROM Virginia; a further account of Bacon's rebellion reproduced in facsimile with an intro. by Thomas P. Abernethy. Charlottesville, Va., 1943. 16 p.

A NARRATIVE OF the Indian and civil wars in Virginia, in the years 1675 and 1676. In: Force tracts, v. 1, no. 11. 47 p.

A corrected version published in 1867 with title: The history of Bacon's and Ingram's rebellion.

A TRUE NARRATIVE of the rise, progress, and cessation of the late rebellion in Virginia, most humbly and impartially reported by his Majestyes commissioners appointed to enquire into the affaires of the said colony [signed by John Berry and Francis Moryson]. Va. mag., 6 (1896), 117-54.

Reprinted: Andrews, Narratives of the insurrections, p. 105-141.

VIRGINIAS DEPLOURED CONDITION; or an impartiall narrative of the murders comitted by the Indians there, and of the . . . outrages of Mr. Nathaniell Bacon, Junr., 1676. Mass. hist. soc., Collections (ser. 4), 9 (1871), 162-76.

WERTENBAKER, THOMAS J. (ed.) The Virginia charter of 1676. Va. Mag., 56 (1948), 263-266.

ARTICLES OF PEACE between the most serene and mighty prince Charles II . . . and several Indian kings and queens, &c. Concluded the 29th day of May, 1677. London, 1677. 18 p.

Reprinted: Va. mag., 14 (1907), 289-96.

MOST EXCELLENT MAJESTY. 1677. [A treaty between the colony of Virginia and several Indian tribes.] [Boston, 1940] 18 p. (Photostat Americana, ser. 2, no. 103)

PROPOSALS IN REGARD to Virginia [1677]. Va. mag., 25 (1917), 71-74.

STRANGE NEWS FROM Virginia; being a full and true account of the life and death of Nathanael Bacon Esquire, who was the only cause and original of all the late troubles in that country. With a full relation of all the accidents which have happened in the late war there between the Christians and Indians. London, 1677. 8 p.

1680-1689

BANISTER, JOHN. Some observations concerning insects made in Virginia, A.D. 1680, with remarks on them by Mr. James Petiver. Royal society of London, Philos. trans., no. 270, March-April, 1701, p. 807-814.

GODWIN, MORGAN. The Negro's & Indians advocate suing for their admission into the church: for a persuasive to the instructing and baptizing of the Negro's and Indians in our plantations. . . . To which is added, a brief account of religion in Virginia. London, 1680. 174 p.

JONES, LEWIS H. Some recently discovered data relating to Capt Roger Jones who came to the colony of Virginia with Lord Culpeper in 1680, including several letters written by him while a captain in the British navy. W & M quar. (ser. 1), 27 (1918), 1-18.

THE VAIN PRODIGAL life, and tragical penitent death of Thomas Hellier . . . who for murdering his master, mistress and a maid, was executed according to law at Westover in Charles City, in the country of Virginia. London, 1680. 40 p.

GODWIN, MORGAN. A supplement to the Negro's & Indians advocate: or, Some further considerations and proposals for

69

the effectual and speedy carrying of the Negro's Christianity in our plantations . . . London, 1681. 12 p.

[PURVIS, JOHN] A complete collection of all laws of Virginia now in force. London [1684?] 300 p.

BYRD, WILLIAM, 1652-1704. Capt. Byrd's letters [1683-1685]. Va. hist. register, 1 (1848), 60-66, 114-19; 2 (1849), 78-83, 203-9.

_____Letters of William Byrd, first [1685]. Va. mag., 24 (1916), 225-37; continued to 28 (1920), 11-25.

GODWIN, MORGAN. Trade preferred before religion, and Christ made to give place to mammon: represented in a sermon relating to the plantations. London, 1685. 34 p.

[DURAND, ―― of Dauphiné] A Huguenot exile in Virginia; or, Voyages of a Frenchman exiled for his religion [1687] . . . introduction and notes by Gilbert Chinard. N. Y., 1934. 189 p.
    Portions printed earlier [Richmond] 1923. 146 p.

CLAYTON, JOHN. A letter . . . to Dr. Grew, in answer to several queries relating to Virginia, sent to him by that learned gentleman, 1687. Royal society of London, Philos. trans., 41 (1739), 143-62.

_____John Clayton [to Dr. Grew(?), April 24, 1684]. W & M quar. (ser. 2), 1 (1921), 114-15.

CUSTIS, JOHN (1653-1713). Letters of John Custis, 1687. Colonial soc. Mass. Publications, 19 (1918), 367-79.

PAGE, JOHN. A deed of gift to my dear son, Captain Matt. Page, one of his Majesty's justices for New Kent county, in Virginia. 1687. Philadelphia, 1856. 276 p.

CLAYTON, JOHN. A letter . . . to the Royal society, May 12, 1688, giving an account of several observables in Virginia, and in his voyage thither, more particularly concerning the air. Mr. Clayton's second letter, containing his farther observations in Virginia. A continuation of Mr. John Clayton's account of Virginia. His letter to the Royal society giving a farther account of the soil, and other observables of Virginia. A continuation of Mr. Clayton's account of Virginia. In: Edmund Halley, Miscellanea curiosa, 2nd ed., London, 1723, v. 3, p. 281-355.

Reprinted: Force tracts, v. 3, no. 12. 45 p.

JAMES II. King of Great Britain. Septima pars patentium de anno regni regis Jacobi Secundi quarto, Sept. 27, [1688]. [Reaffirming the grant of the Northern Neck in Virginia to Lord Culpeper.] [London? 1688] 6 p.

1690-1699

BANISTER, JOHN. The extracts of four letters [from Virginia, 1668-1692] to Dr. Lister, communicated by him to the publisher. Royal society of London, Philos. trans., no. 198, March 1693, p. 667-72.

[LUDWELL, PHILIP] An alphabeticall abridgment of the laws of Virginia [prepared in 1694]. Va. mag., 9 (1902), 273-88; continued to 10 (1903), 241-54.

RUDMAN, REV. ANDREW JOHN. Diary of Rev. Andrew Rudman, July 25, 1696—June 14, 1697; ed. by Luther Anderson. German American annals, 8 (1906), 282-312; continued to 9 (1907), 9-18.

AN ESSAY UPON THE government of the English plantations on the continent of America (1701). An anonymous Virginian's proposals for liberty under the British crown, with two memoranda by William Byrd. Ed. by Louis B. Wright. San Marino, Calif., 1945. 66 p.

VIRGINIA. Acts of assembly, passed in the colony of Virginia, from 1662, to 1715. v. 1. London, 1727. 391 p.

BYRD, WILLIAM. The writings of Colonel William Byrd of Westover in Virginia, esqr.; ed. by John S. Bassett. N. Y., 1901. 461 p.

www.ingramcontent.com/pod-product-compliance
Lightning Source LLC
Chambersburg PA
CBHW071233290326
41931CB00037B/2869